I GOT

IT

BACK!

Book Cover Design: Lock It! Graphics
Photography by Jesse Hamble-www.jessehamble.com

Scripture quotations marked NLT are taken from the Holy Bible, New Living Translation copyright 1996. Used by permission of Tyndale House Publishers, Inc., Wheaton, Illinois, 60189. All rights reserved.

Scripture taken from the HOLY BIBLE, NEW INTERNATIONAL VERSION. Copyright © 1973, 1978, 1984 International Bible Society. Used by permission of Zondervan. All rights reserved.

Scripture taken from The Message. Copyright © 1994, 1995, 1996, 2000, 2001, 2002. Used by permission of NavPress Publishing Group.

Scripture quotations taken from the Amplified Bible, copyright © 1954, 1962, 1964, 1965, 1987 by the Lockman Foundation. Used by permission. (www.Lockman.org)

Words of "Sometimes Miracles Hide' permission given by Bruce Carroll - www. brucecarroll.com

Published by
Serenity Publishing & Communications, Inc.
www.serenitypcinc.com

Editor: Monica Link

ISBN: 0-9788007-9-6

PREFACE
INTRODUCTION

DEDICATION

I dedicate this book to
Gloria–we made it through the rain!

Candice, Dionne, Kim, Lyric, Sean,
(and Baby on the way.)

Take the baton and run with it.
You are my rewards!

PREFACE

I remember sitting in the lobby of a hotel in New Orleans, Louisana approximately five years ago in a meeting with Alvin and a representative from a major book publisher. We discussed the possibilities of him writing a book. It was exciting to think that Alvin was going to have the opportunity to write about how we rebounded from desolation and despair.

Every hotel receipt, every airline ticket jacket and pieces of paper he could find summed up visions, dreams and mini messages from the corner of his mind. They were everywhere. Alvin had thousands of pieces of paper that could have easily been translated into a book, but the time was not yet. He decided, "I'm not ready to write a book." The dream was put on the shelf and we went on with our lives singing, teaching, ministering and doing the work of the Kingdom until we came to a crossroads in October 2004. The events that took place propelled us into a new season. A season of *I Got It Back!*

If there ever was a time that this book is needed in the body of Christ that time is now. *I Got It Back!* is a powerful tool that has been written to prepare God's people for the Faith Life. This book is filled with life experiences and practical tools for those who have given their power away to others, to once and for all "get it back".

I Got It Back!

Alvin, I was so confident that you were more than capable and qualified to present a stunning and powerful piece of work for God's Kingdom and you delivered. You have only just begun.

Your Partner for Life,
Gloria

INTRODUCTION

Alright, stop pretending everything is ok. Quit acting like you have it all together! You don't and the great news is that you don't have to. The frustration and pressure that you are feeling may be coming at you from many different directions. The truth is, your life doesn't have to be stuck in neutral because what you dreamed about, hoped for, and even prayed for, didn't turn out the way you expected.

The reason why I am writing this book is because I have been there too. Paralyzed emotionally and spiritually to the point that even though I sort of knew what I needed to do to make things better, I just didn't have the heart, the faith, the fire in my soul to do anything about it.

I'm writing this book because a high five, a hallelujah, three songs, three points and a conclusion will no longer do. I'm also writing this book because I guess I'm a little selfish. In my lifetime, I've discovered that when you help make someone else's existence a little better, you start to feel a little better about your own existence. When you give the gift of spiritual peace away to others I have found that more spiritual peace will come your way.

I know that there are many people writing books that speak of empowerment. However, I wrote this book because what was once my passion has now become my burden. There are too many people that have retreated into the back seat of their life. They wait for God, wait for other people, wait for a stroke of good luck to give them the power that they already possess; but have sadly given it away. Now is the time for you to face the truth. It's time to confront your issues, follow your heart and find your peace of mind.

Maybe a story that I share or an experience I have had will identify with you. You see, by the time I was thirty-four years old, I had two children out of wedlock, sixteen jobs (failed at most of them), two apartment evictions, one home foreclosure, two bankruptcies and very serious marriage problems. I most certainly don't mean to boast, but today by God's grace I've been in business and ministry successfully for sixteen years, married to my childhood sweetheart for twenty-eight years, have traveled the world and have had my mind expanded from the experiences of my life as well as observing other peoples lives and cultures. I've learned how to seek wisdom. Simply put wisdom is the ability to solve a problem.

You see, I've lost a lot...but I got it back and you will too! At times I feel like an imbedded reporter and a soldier in the battleground of life. I am also aware that there are still more challenges ahead for you and me. So I pray this book will be a tool in your arsenal to overcome the challenges of today as well as the ones we will face tomorrow.

Maybe you've read all the books in the library about empowerment, and for whatever reason you are still feeling powerless. You've memorized Bible verses and listened to teaching CDs, but your mind is still disconnected from your heart and your spirit. Well, if I may be so bold, should you choose to receive it, I'm telling you that now is your appointed time. Where the light comes on. The ministering angel lifts up your head. The natural holds hands with the supernatural. God's power becomes your power. That's why you're reading this book. You do realize that the same power that raised Christ from the dead resides inside of you? Did you give it away? Well, it's time to get your power back!

Be warned that some of the things you are about to read in this book may unsettle you, make you uncomfortable, or defy what you've always imagined to be true. For your sake, I hope it does. The greatest journey is to find the real truth of God's love for us and His power in us. Who does He say I am? How does He say I should live? Why does He say I'm here? Inquiring hearts want to know.

The fact is that many of us have received, well let's just say, not the best teaching or preaching. Or perhaps none at all when it comes to real life problems and affairs of the heart. Yet others have received half-truths which are nothing more than lies dressed in white garments. If that's the case, then it's time for us to discover the truths that help us to know our true passion, our unique voice, our hope restored, and strength renewed. It's time to get our power back!

You see, while there are many other books that are teaching you to take control of your situations, I take the stand that you need to take control of you! So instead of me sitting down and wishing that I could in a sense reach each of you personally, I decided to attempt to reach as many as I can through this book. Sure, I could have hosted a conference to see who would readjust their lives to attend. But, I decided that this written form would be my way of making a formal introduction to the people who are looking for another perspective.

Let me tell you what the challenge of writing this book is. I am consumed by the content that I am presenting to you. The challenge that lies before me is to convey the tender strings of my heart while throwing a rope of rescue to those who have need of what I have to say. In this book there will be many stories from many time spans, experienced by several people, yet the truth, sometimes the hard truth will need to be given in order that we, yes we, can get to where we are going.

Let me give you a hint that you are the person that should be reading this book. If you're feeling overwhelmed by life, and everything that could be shaken has been shaken, then this is the book for you. Perhaps everything seems to be going well, and you're grateful for the many blessings of your life, but yet, something is still missing. Well, this book is for you too.

I know it is easy to say, "Get up!" "Take control!" But you and I know that words alone are not enough. You have gone far beyond head knowledge. You know *what* to do – but perhaps you don't want to admit that you don't know *how* to do it. You know that you need nothing short of an angel to pull you up from the pit of your life at this point.

This is not the book to feed your pain or soothe your sadness to the point that you continue in a defeated posture of impotence in your life. This is the book to jolt you into a posture that won't let you stay in the same place with the same mindset. Come on, let's do this together. Let's confront and take back the power that we gave up to vices and other people. Get up and stand on your feet, go after your power and don't stop until you get it back!

Chapter One
LET'S SET THE RECORD STRAIGHT

This is not easy for me to confess. It never is when you finally realize that what you prayed about, got frustrated about, almost threw in the towel about and blamed God for was something that was never going to happen for you anyway. Well, not in the way you wanted it to happen. No matter how frustrated you got, no matter how hard you prayed.

For over 20 years, I prayed to God that He would take away all of my fears. I could be an inspiring author, a persuasive negotiator, an award winning songwriter, a successful entrepreneur, a dynamic speaker or perhaps even a respected humanitarian or a fearless leader.

Actually, I wouldn't have minded being comfortable in my own skin. Secure in my own opinions and decisions. If only I didn't freeze up and retreat back to what I was, instead of pressing on to what I could be. I kept finding myself rehearsing all the consequences and the pitfalls of my probable failures in my mind. I didn't say potential success. I said probable failure.

With this mindset, I was doomed from the moment I got out of bed. What a horrible way to live. I was a dreamer with no strategy. Eventually...even the dreams died. When dreams die, in a sense, at least spiritually, you cease to exist. You see, God didn't just up and take my fears away. Well, not in the way I thought He would.

Heaven knows I'm not alone in this. If you were to offer me 20 million shares of prime blue chip stock, versus one dollar for every person who never reached their God given potential because they were waiting for the right feeling to hit them, needless to say, I'd choose the one-dollar deal.

Maybe your fear is coming at you from a different direction. Why would anyone stay in an abusive relationship? Why do we fly off the handle when we feel the least bit offended? Why do we blame the boss, the church, our spouse, and our parents for the mess we're in presently?

The truth is that they just might be the reason why you feel the way you do. They may be the cause of what is seemingly holding you back. For as many who have been stuck, there are also those who found a way to find the strength and boldness to break away from a defeating attitude, a defeating lifestyle and the influence of negative people.

We live outward fake lives. Psalm 119:29 says, *"Lord, keep me from lying to myself."* You lie to yourself when you live other people's truths and not your own. Let's dispel a few of the lies that keep us deceiving ourselves and walking in fear.

Myth 1- If I truly have faith, I shouldn't feel afraid.
Truth – Yes you will! Being afraid isn't really the problem here. Some fears are learned unhealthy fears. Others are protective healthy fears. For example, if I'm walking down the road and I see a 600-pound bear coming my way. Now, that just might be a healthy fear!

I was once told that if you should happen to come upon a bear and he's too close for you to run away, you should fall to the ground, curl up in a fetal position and play dead. (I sure hope you'll never need to use this tactic.) Bears don't see well. If you take the submissive position, you won't seem threatening to the bear and maybe he'll just go away. Now on the other hand, if the bear is really hungry...

It is how you react to fear that is important. In the book of Ephesians 6:19-20, Paul asked for the people to pray that he would have boldness in the face of fear when preaching the gospel. Paul faced rejection, physical beating, imprisonment and even death. When I read that, the lights came on for me. Fear is not just a plague of the timid. Even the great have fears. If someone as great as the Apostle Paul had fear yet accomplished powerful things for God, then there's no shame that I have fears too. Greatness is not just determined by a great feat or deed accomplished. It is also determined by the fact that you have to wade through the raging waters of fear to get to the other side.

17

God doesn't necessarily take our fears away, but He will give us boldness to walk through our fears. I hate it when super religious people make you feel like a second class Christian because you fear something that they don't. I agree with the quote "there is nothing to fear but fear itself." That may be true, but it still doesn't make me feel any better!

There is another thing to know about being afraid. The more secure you feel in making good decisions, the less afraid you'll feel. Seek wise counsel from people who have experience or a great and compassionate understanding in the area of your fear. Most people I speak to get advice from unqualified friends, family or anyone who is glib, opinionated and talks a good line. And when you do get sound advice, do it. A lot of people only hear what they want to hear, but won't do what they ought to do. Don't fall into this trap, because if you do, you're just lying to yourself.

Lastly, don't become a wishful thinker. Wishful thinkers spend time hoping things will work out, not getting wisdom. They make irrational decisions and don't take action. Faith isn't foolishness nor is it a shot in the dark. The Bible says, *"In all your getting, get understanding."* (Proverbs 4:7) We live in a world where someone has probably been where you've been. If we ask, seek and knock, we will find a *"lamp unto our feet and a light unto our path"* (Psalm 119:105) that at the very least will help us navigate through the situations of our life.

Myth 2 - I'm not worthy.
Truth – Well, God says you are! (Psalm 139:14)
Some of us grew up in churches where at one time
or the other someone may have prayed, "Oh God,
I'm not worthy of your goodness." Maybe you thought
humility was to put yourself down, so that you didn't
seem like you were too boastful. Others of us have
endured physical or emotional abuse by someone
we trusted or cared about. While still others may not
have succeeded at anything in life so they
have resigned to a life of mediocrity.

I have a supportive family and a career to die
for. I live in the land of opportunity, and I possess a
glorious faith that was given to me as a gift from
God. Yet, I haven't always been the best husband,
father, son or brother. I'm not the best singer in the
world. (I'm not the worst either!) I sometimes take
for granted some of the simplest yet most profound
blessings in life. Like the life sustaining air I breathe,
or the vibrant beauty of the landscape that surrounds
me as the seasons change here in the Northeast.

My children are heirs of all that my wife and I
have now or will possess. Should we die before them,
they get the proverbial "farm". They didn't work for
it. They may not even be entitled to it, but they are
my children. Whatever I declare is mine, whether
they were born out of the union of Gloria and I, or
whether through adoption, they are also declared
worthy.

You have a God who loves you absolutely, unconditionally and desires fellowship and communication with you. Jesus' death on the cross and resurrection from the dead signifies that He paid the ultimate sacrifice for me with His life. That's how much I'm worth to Him. He paid a ransom for me that with time or money, I could have never paid. In Jeremiah 29:11, God says that His plans for me are to give me a hope and a future. I mean God Himself has actual plans for me! And you see even when my natural body dies, He said that my soul, the real me, would have an eternal home with Him where I'll never die.

You and I did absolutely nothing to earn all of this. I'm just one out of the billions of souls on this planet. But you know what, when I sing to Him, I believe He sees just an audience of one. All I ever did was accept His love and ask the Spirit into my life. That's it. Amazing!

When you say I'm not worthy, you tell God that you're more informed than He is. He wasted His time in creating you higher than the animals and that His death on the cross for you was a waste of His shed blood. He must have had an off day. Listen, not one of us may be entitled to any of the promises of God, but we're worthy. This is not for you to intellectually understand. Just receive it. By faith...just receive it.

Myth 3- I can't face rejection.
Truth–*"Be strong in the Lord, and in the power of His might."* (Eph. 6:10) Rejection is a part of life.

Much of my fear stemmed from wanting everybody's approval. When I was a kid in grade school, I remember a bunch of us guys were in the school gym during gym class. As a chubby (do they still use that word?), bonafide dork, I gravitated over to the basketball court, where the cool guys were. I thought this might give me a chance to connect with some of the jocks and by osmosis, maybe some of their "cool" would rub off on me. Ahhh, I could be a ladies man! Super Fly...you know what I'm sayin', just trying to get over! I had a couple of things going against me, but I felt like today they're gonna cut a brotha' some slack. (Please excuse me and indulge my early seventies vernacular.)

I already told you I was a chubby dork. I also had another reputation I wasn't so fond of at the time either. There was a pretty red-haired African American girl, with freckles no less that was a Jehovah's Witness. I was a choirboy Bapticostal (part Baptist, part Pentecostal...long story). No cussing, no dancing, no hanging out with the wrong crowd and a whole lot of going to church. The other kids called us "church kids incorporated." My how I loathed that title! Well it's time to break that mold and get my "hoops on" with the fellas.

Nine guys loomed under the basketball net and two team captains were chosen. Then the captains chose who would be on their team. "I'll take Freddy." "Then I'll take Louie." "I'll take Bobby." So I'll take Oscar." "I'll take Big Mike." I'm praying, "Please God let him pick me. If You love me, he'll pick me. I'll keep my room clean. I'll get straight A's if he picks me."

"I'll pick...Lenny." My heart dropped like a plane crashing from 35,000 feet. They headed off to the foul line, while I just laughed and said, "Hey guys, catch you next game." But inside I knew there would never be a next game... and there never was.

I don't know if my fear of rejection, my seeking everybody's approval, started there on the basketball court or was just solidified there. I do know that I spent the next twenty or so years battling low self-esteem and people pleasing. That gym class experience eventually made it's way into other areas of my life and decisions.

I hated rejection back then and I hate rejection now. I have since resolved that issue. Just because I may not be the right size, have the right education, be the right color or the right whatever, I absolutely will not be denied. I've learned to value my own opinion and sense of worth. We all have "stuff" in our lives that needs fixing. Some "stuff" is more apparent than others, but it's still "stuff" all the same. I welcome constructive criticism from a very, very (count them on two hands) small circle of professionals, pastors and loved ones who truly know and care about me. But certainly not from every Tom, Dick and Harry, and certainly not from some self-righteous, holier than thou, ill informed, egotistical, full of himself, don't know when to shut up, know it all! (Whew, I feel better now! You should try saying that.)

This is not to say that they're not right, but if every time I see you, you point out my shortcomings, all you're going to do is make me angry, not make me better. I may already be feeling horrible about myself. There are some things you say to me, and sometimes you pray for me, and sometimes you do both.

Many of our issues are the result of a deeper problem. That's why New Year's resolutions and diets usually don't work. You must find your inner strength. My strength and confidence comes from God, and He's still not finished with me yet. He's still working on me, but, He's also still working through me.

I'm finding that self-confidence is useless. It is limited to the extent of what I think of my achievements or myself. God confidence is everything because in Him there are no limits. You don't have to play head games or only depend on who you are, but on the full force of the promises of God and He cannot lie.

Myth 4- I'm not a strong person
Truth – Just because you're imperfect doesn't mean you're powerless. We are all imperfect in some way. Being strong really means becoming strong. None of us are born strong.

Babies are weak and fragile and must be cared for. Over a period of time a baby starts using his or her little fingers and legs. He or she drinks milk and eats the right food to nourish his or her little eyes and teeth.

The first time they fall and bump their head, they cry for their mama. After the tenth time of falling, they just shake it off, and get going again. Walking turns into running, and before you know it, what's not nailed down will be tossed down!

Later in this chapter I'm going to cover how to become a strong person.

Myth 5 – I don't know what to do.
Truth – Get connected to the Source who is the Spirit. Seek wise counsel. Don't live in a vacuum! Many times when faced with fear, we retreat into ourselves. The answer may not be inside of you, but outside of you.

Many years ago I owed the IRS a lot of money. A business failure along with ignorance on my own part, brought me to the point of tremendous stress and serious insomnia. I didn't think I'd ever be free from this mountain of debt with interest accruing daily.

One day as I drove to an appointment in the city, I was so distressed, I could barely think straight. I started praying that God would somehow supernaturally erase my debt. (A tactic preached by many ignorant or quack preachers in order to raise money. At that time I succumbed to the same illusion.) A rich benefactor. A check in the mail. A computer mysteriously erases my little problem. I'm not denying that this hasn't happened, because it has happened to me but the chances are about the same as you hitting the lottery. Besides, if God can supernaturally make your debts go away,

24

why can't He supernaturally give you the ideas or plan to live up to your responsibilities?

I turned on the radio to listen to some music but I didn't seem to be in the mood for music, Gospel or otherwise that day, so I turned the radio off. I began to pray and say, "Father, would you help me. Give me a plan or an idea. I'm not asking you to take it all away because some of the debt was justifiably owed to the government. With the high rate of interest and penalties constantly building up, I'll be ninety years old before I can see the light of day."

Just then, in my spirit I heard, "turn on the radio." Not an actual voice, but like you hear a melody playing in your head, I heard it again, "turn on the radio." I just had it on and just wasn't feeling music today, but I turned on the music station anyway. For "some reason," I felt compelled to keep searching and searching until I landed on a radio program where an author was being interviewed about a book he had written on how to deal with tax problems.

Well I almost had a car accident! I couldn't believe it. This author was speaking like he was talking to me. As soon as I returned home later that day, I bought a money order (I didn't have a credit card) and immediately put it in the mail and ordered the book. (Note: The title and author of the book is being withheld. Since that was in the early nineties,there have been changes to the tax laws. Seek advice from a qualified professional.)

I used the principles I learned from the book to greatly reduce some of the unjustified debt. I was then able to set up a payment plan that I could reasonably pay. This was amazing to me because I couldn't afford an attorney at the time and most of the other books I looked at were filled with so much legal terminology that it could have just as well been written in Greek.

Listen for the still small voice. Look at the billboards along the way. I don't know what your answer is today, but there is always, always, always an answer. You may not receive your answer today. So then for you there is peace.

Don't worry about anything; instead pray about everything. Tell God what you need, and thank Him for all He has done. If you do this you will experience God's peace, which is far more wonderful than the human mind can understand. His peace will guide your hearts and mind as you live in Christ Jesus. (Phil: 4:6-8)

Myth 6 - I'll be misunderstood.
Truth – Now, this is true. You weren't put on this earth to win popularity contests. That's for beauty pageants. This is real life. Your first priority is you. We spend way too much time allowing other people to control us. You've got to learn to put your foot down, lift your head up and stop letting other people control and manipulate you. Everybody's not going to like you no matter how hard you try anyway. So you might as well get to loving yourself.

26

The first step to overcoming fear is to see your greatness. Mother Teresa is great because she was selfless. She founded The Missionaries of Charity, whose primary task was to love and care for those persons whom nobody else was prepared to look after. Nelson Mandela is great because he worked for peace and stood against racism. He spent twenty-seven years in prison for a worthy cause. Mr. Mandela said, "Sometimes it takes about a generation to be great. You can be that great generation."

The day you understand that every great person has had to walk the plank of fear to get to the other side of a life fulfilled is the day you sign your personal emancipation proclamation.

God didn't give us a spirit of fear; but of power and of love and of a sound mind. (2 Timothy 1:7) God doesn't just remove your fears. You remove them! You've got the power. God will give you the courage and boldness to walk through your fears. So use your faith and rely on God for the courage you need to make it through. We all have it in different measures, but we all have it. It is a gift from God. Don't confuse faith with wishful thinking. Wishful thinking has no true basis for a triumphant ending. It's like romancing a movie star you'll never meet. It's all in your fantasies. Now, the object of your faith may be far fetched, with all odds against you. You might be in need of a miracle. But as faith is a gift from God, the foundation of true faith is rooted in God. Stay connected with the Source. As we are joined with Christ , we will receive the heart and mind of the Spirit. He will direct us in how we are to believe and what to believe for.

I want to make one thing clear. I used to believe that doubt was the opposite of faith. But I don't believe that any longer. In my further study of the Bible, I believe the opposite of faith is indecision. Thomas doubted when he saw the resurrected Christ. But when He placed his hand in the pierced side of Jesus he worshipped Him. On the other hand, Judas' indecisiveness caused Him to betray Christ for money and what he could buy with it. He later died a tragic death.

Real faith is strong – not weak because God is strong. Fear makes an impact on your life by paralyzing you from living out the truth of your life. Some people say, "Don't acknowledge that you have fears. This gives the devil a place to move in your life." This is another lie you tell yourself. What gives the devil a place in your life is when you allow your fears to stop you from moving forward and you stop living with focus and passion. Do you see yourself in any of the following?

FEAR OF FAILURE
You can't move ahead or make a sound decision because things probably won't work out. You see all failure as fatal. No rebounds...this is the end of the road.

FEAR OF REJECTION
You can't risk loving or putting your feelings on the line. You've been crushed before and it's not going to happen again. You sabotage any remote chance of healthy relationships. Or you may be needy and clingy and will do anything to be accepted.

FEAR OF NOT BEING SUCCESSFUL

You don't try any harder than you have to because you can't bear the thought of not achieving your desired goal. So you just stay where you are, making excuses and convincing yourself that where you are now is just fine.

FEAR OF SUCCESS

Let me dwell on this for a moment. For years the fear of success caused me to avoid things that would have brought the ministry and things I'm passionate about to a stronger more impacting position. I didn't give 100% to expanding the reach of my ministry in the United States and around the world. If you asked me why, the answer I would have given you at one time was complex but today it is quite simple. The more successful you are, the more visible you are. The more visible you are the more of a target you are.

I didn't want my actions being scrutinized or misunderstood. I didn't want my sometimes controversial opinions and ideas to be challenged or taken out of context. I wanted to be seen as someone who goes with the flow and not someone who shakes things up. Nobody wants a singer with an opinion. Just shut up and sing! I thought I'd spend too much time defending myself. Perhaps the ministry would suffer and the finances would be affected.

I was not sure I could pay that price. I really liked being liked by people (at least I thought I was) and I made every effort not to change my likeability factor. After all, if I started saying things that are controversial then where would that put me?

I subconsciously and at times consciously hindered my success because I was closed-minded and didn't take advantage of some of the resources available for me to further my success. Here's the thing, I was also refusing to impact the people that God wanted me to, because I was committed to just staying under the radar.

Today, things are different because my view of who I am changed and what I should be doing to impact my world. Success is not a curse. Success is an opportunity to do more with more. Whether that success comes as influence, fame, money, or a combination of them all. Being successful has a price, but then again everything does. As the opportunities present themselves ..dare to be great! You can literally make a profound impact in somebody's life today. Launch out into the deep and let your faith take you somewhere that you've never been before.

BASIC TRAINING FOR OVERCOMING FEAR

"Be strong in the Lord and in the power of His might." (Ephesians 6:10) This strength comes from the supernatural power of God. Not your strength. Too many people think that going to church on Sunday, listening to sermons, playing Christian music and even reading the Bible in and of itself is enough.

God doesn't just want us to feel inspired. He wants us to be transformed by having our minds renewed. The mind is the battleground where fear and depression germinate. It is also the place where we can begin to see the truth of who God is and who we are in Him. True worship will equip us as well as change us into the image of the Father. How futile it is to be stirred, but not changed.

Take responsibility for your own life.

Because you have been a victim does not mean that you have to make that your permanent residence in life. When you dwell on what used to be or how bad you've been mistreated, you've turned into your own worst enemy. You've become the victim as well as the predator. It means you refuse to take responsibility for your actions. Remember, you can't change what you don't acknowledge.

Personal growth is the key to prosperity.

It's amazing that some of us invest more in a car or television than we spend in developing our minds. Many years ago, I used to sell shop at home carpet in the apartments and homes of some of the poorest, most crime ridden neighborhoods in New York City. The company advertised a low grade, inexpensive carpet. When the appointment was set up with the prospective buyer, they were told the salesman would also have samples of other grades of carpet.

I would enter customer's living rooms and to my surprise, some places had just a bulb hanging from an exposed wire in the ceiling, but no lamps. I measured bedrooms for carpet, where there was no mattress, bed frame, dresser, or lamps. Just a box spring on the floor and a few boxes scattered with clothes.

31

There were many times, however, a beautiful big screen television, (which I found out later, can be rented). In all the time I sold carpet, I never, ever sold the inexpensive carpet. They always chose the more expensive grade and would pay with a couple thousand dollars cash from a box hidden in a back room somewhere. The truth is, I understand the irony of this. When you feel stuck, fearful and hopeless, you begin to pacify yourself with things that make you feel better. But this is only temporary satisfaction. This money could have been spent to invest in a vocational course, buy some books, or jumpstart higher education.

You owe it to yourself to read the stories of other great people, just like you. Those who endured and prospered in the face of desperate situations. Oprah Winfrey has no doubt inspired millions of viewers, including myself. Maybe you know the story of Tyler Perry who recounts how he slept in his car as an adult and endured abuse growing up to become one of the most successful directors, producers and writers of this decade. I once heard a great saying. *"Wealthy people have big libraries. Poor people have big televisions."*

Find a mentor. Take free courses online. Read books to inspire you and take your mind out of the four corners of your own little world. New and fresh ideas will begin to take shape in your mind and the blessings will begin to flow as you begin to act on this newfound knowledge.

Learn how to communicate effectively with others.

Learning how to get your point across and negotiating your desires will give you a feeling of accomplishment and empowerment in a job situation, as an entrepreneur or in a personal relationship. When you can't put the right words together to say how you feel, or when in a confrontational situation you will always feel like you're on the losing side. Everybody hates being a loser, so once again fear raises it's ugly head.

I love to listen to great preachers like T.D. Jakes, Joyce Meyer, Dr. David Ireland and Joel Osteen who so effectively communicate about dealing with ourselves and others in a Godly way. Even the manner in which they preach is a lesson in effective communication. That's why their audiences number are in the millions.

Proverbs 18:20-21 says that *"Words satisfy the soul as food satisfies the stomach; the right words on a person's lips bring satisfaction. Those who love to talk will experience the consequences, for the tongue can kill or nourish life."*

GET HELP!

When all else fails, there is still help to walk you through your fears. Don't isolate yourself, but insulate yourself. There are great churches or counseling centers in many cities that offer free counseling or they can point you in the right direction.

The Internet may lead you to accredited and licensed individuals and programs that can help you walk out of the valley of fear you're in. If you're being hurt, you must tell somebody today! Talking is the process that opens the door to resolution.

A couple near and dear to my heart, have been having serious marriage problems for years. They never told a soul, not even anyone that could help. By the time I found out about how bad their situation was, a wall of anger, resentment, and hatred built up so strong that it didn't look like it could be penetrated. I don't know what the outcome of their situation will be, but when they found out they couldn't work it out by themselves, they should have sought help and persisted until they found the right source that they could trust and work with.

God doesn't always take away your fears. But He'll give you courage and boldness to confront and walk through them!

Chapter Two

DEEPENING YOUR RELATIONSHIP WITH GOD

In misery she laid in her bed with a painful and debilitating spinal condition. She had worked hard and educated herself to achieve her dream of teaching in the public schools of Philadelphia. But now her career screeched to a halting end because a reckless student struck her with a piece of slate. Her name was Eliza Hewitt. She had every right to be angry and bitter. Instead, she filled her days studying English literature. She also began to sing and write:

Sing the wondrous love of Jesus
Sing His mercy and His grace
In the mansions bright and blessed
He'll prepare for us a place

Professor John Sweeney got a hold of her writing and requested she write more. They began to collaborate and he set music to some of her lyrics. Over 50 hymns flowed from her pen and into the hearts of churchgoers across America. Had Eliza never been bedridden, she might not have written some of the greatest hymns that have ever been sung through the years.

Although she died in 1920, many of us baby boomers still remember such songs as "My Faith Has Found A Resting Place," "When We All Get to Heaven" and "More About Jesus"

The life of a Christian is not exempt from tragedy. You might have experienced an unfortunate divorce, the death of a child or a bad report from the doctor. In all of these things, the life of a Christian is not meant to be lived in constant worry or defeat because of circumstances. This sounds like an oxymoron – devastating tragedy, yet the peace of God. Our world at times seems to be spinning out of control, yet believing that God is in control. In the natural, it makes no sense. Our emotional responses to the problems of life can overwhelm us. That's why it's so important to deepen your relationship with God.

When we are strong in the Lord and His mighty power we become anchored to God in spite of our thoughts, emotions, and circumstances. The Christian life is a life led by the Spirit. Christians don't live by coincidence. Everything that happens in the life of the believer whether good or bad should ultimately draw us closer to Christ and bring glory to His name. We are ambassadors of Christ, building His kingdom here on earth.

So if you love God, know scripture and go to church every Sunday, then this chapter is for you. But if you do all those things and something is still missing, then this chapter is for you too. Oh, by the way– to the ones who are looking for more substance in their spiritual search than just a few songs and a sermon, we've also got you covered.

Ever hear a preacher speaking real loud, but saying nothing or rattling off a bunch of cliches? I once heard a preacher who was looking for a few amens from the congregation say "ya'll ain't saying nothing to me!"

Quite frankly I was thinking, "neither are you!" I find way too many unqualified, self-appointed Bishops and Pastors who through a little charisma and a lot of self confidence, have misled people. Preaching half truths that draw people to themselves or a form of godliness, instead of leading them to Jesus.

We should have the utmost respect for our Christian leaders, but we must know and understand what the Bible says for ourselves so we're not swayed by every teaching and doctrine that comes our way. We should never become more enamored with the messenger than we are with the One the message is supposed to be about.

Many times I've heard preachers say that if you just give in the offering, God's going to give you a promotion on your job, and He's going to cancel all of your debts and He's going to heal your sickness. Just plant your seed.

But any good farmer will tell you that you just don't go around just throwing seeds on the ground. You've got to prepare and till the soil. You must fertilize the soil and remove the weeds. The seeds in the soil must be watered. In other words, financial prosperity does not come by putting money in the offering basket alone. There are some things that you must do.

Sometimes I wish I could just send out money to ministries, stay home, watch television and let the mailman bring checks to me everyday. These kind of blanket statements are irresponsible and preposterous. Yes, we are supposed to give into the work of the Lord, but that's not the whole truth. If you don't understand the proper use of money, it leads to misuse. High interest debt, spending more than you earn, no savings or investment plan and not putting God first when it comes to your money will keep you in bondage no matter how richly God blesses you. (More about giving in another chapter.) To have a deeper relationship with God, we must know the truth and the whole truth. There's no need to oversell or undersell God. He is who He is. Period.

I've met too many people that are constantly running from conference to conference, looking for a prophet to give them a word from the Lord. Searching for that magic touch that will beat up the devil and give them instant solutions to their problems. Conferences can be great sources for information and prophecy is Biblical. However, neither one of them are supposed to be a substitute to knowing God for yourself. The Apostle Paul, who was arguably the most influential Christian of the New Testament, suffered greatly because of his faith in God. I believe that qualifies him to say,

"And so, since God in his mercy has given us this wonderful ministry, we never give up. We reject all shameful and underhanded methods. We do not try to trick anyone, and we do not distort the word of God. We tell the truth before God, and all who are honest know that.... We are pressed on every side

by troubles, but we are not crushed and broken. We are perplexed, but we don't give up and quit. We are hunted down, but God never abandons us. We get knocked down, but we get up again and keep going." (2 Corinthians 4:1,2,8,9)

If you're a preacher reading this chapter, this by no means is an attack on you (of which I am proudly one too), who speak the truth in love. I'm talking to those who knowingly and sometimes inadvertently use shameful and underhanded methods as Paul spoke about. As messengers of Christ, we must make sure we're not passing on some flawed doctrine that may have been ignorantly passed down to us even with good intentions.

I love the funny television commercial where a man stands and says with a smile that the website for their insurance company is so easy to use, even a caveman can use it! The scene cuts away to a fancy restaurant, with that same man profusely apologizing over dinner, to a couple of open collared, well-groomed, smartly dressed (yet hairy) cavemen for making that comment. I love one of the annoyed cavemen's response to the apology; "Next time you should do a little research."

God is not calling for us all to be theologians, delving into the original greek, making an exhaustive study of the Byzantine Empire. But when you hear a message preached, don't just take notes and file it away. I think the caveman in the commercial had it right. Next time you should do a little research!

Even if you attend a great church with great leadership, you must still personally take all the good that's been deposited into you and apply it, so that you can serve God and experience the joy of your relationship with Him. It has to be a personal relationship with Christ based on the Word of God. You cannot allow others to control and dictate whether you hear from God or not. "Am I praying enough? What should I do with my life? I'm not fulfilled." The fruit of spiritual control is spiritual immaturity! You will never be strong in your faith by letting others control you or seeking everybody's approval. Your Pastor, your boss, your co-workers and even your family members are not to take the place of your brain.

I don't mean to be harsh, but so what if someone didn't return your phone call! So what no one is paying attention to you! Who cares if people don't get you because you choose to not blend with the crowd! Don't even try to figure it out. It's a waste of time. You don't have to agree with everything someone says just because they say it in a microphone! You need to get your validation from who Jesus says you are.

"Trust in the LORD with all your heart and lean not on your own understanding; in all your ways acknowledge him, and he will make your paths straight." (Proverbs 3:5,6)

God will use your relationship with others to speak into your life, but the ultimate responsibility of how you live your Christian life is up to you.

Get your prayer life back!

When God asks us to pray, He's not calling us to a boring, tedious, repetitive conversation. It shouldn't be as though we are talking to some stuffy distant, uncaring dignitary. When we are talking to the Father, we are talking to someone who richly and deeply cares about our lives. He is not looking to call us on the carpet for every little thing we did or did not do. *"What marvelous love the Father has extended to us! Just look at it--we're called children of God! That's who we really are. But that's also why the world doesn't recognize us or take us seriously, because it has no idea who He is or what He's up to."* (I John 3:1)

Persistent worry is detrimental to the believer because it replaces persistent prayer. Worry doesn't cause God to move. However, God will move heaven and earth when we pray in faith according to His will. (see Luke 18:18)

So then how do we know His will? We know His will by His Spirit. You've got to get rid of your ego, if you truly want to walk in the Spirit. How do you know you're walking in the Spirit and not your ego? I'm glad you asked.

" What happens when we live God's way? He brings gifts into our lives, much the same way that fruit appears in an orchard—things like affection for others, exuberance about life, serenity. We develop a willingness to stick with things, a sense of compassion in the heart, and a conviction that a basic holiness permeates things and people. We find ourselves in-

41

volved in loyal commitments, not needing to force our way in life, able to marshal and direct our energies wisely. Legalism is helpless in bringing this about; it only gets in the way.." (Galatians 5:22–23)

Let's get real though...when you're in the middle of a divorce, your teenagers are acting like aliens from outer space, you're being audited by the IRS and the company you work for is closing because of corporate embezzlement, it's hard to "work up" some fruit.

The way to overcome this is to never, ever let your life get so full that you don't find the time to seek God in prayer and meditation. Your fellowship with other believers is also important so make sure that you have people with a heart after God in your life. Carve out space and a place in your life to daily meet with God. It may be when you're walking at lunchtime. It may be in the car to and from work. It could be sitting in your recliner in the basement. I promise you that if you are constantly feeling like you're losing it, it's because you've put too much distance between you and God. The Bible calls these moments, the secret place. God's voice is amplified as we linger in His presence. This can only be found in the secret place.

Religious praying is useless. Remember, prayer is conversing with God, so forget about style and focus on being transparent. You're not praying useless prayers to an impotent God, but life changing prayers to our all powerful God! (Isaiah 37:15,16) God will open every door that should be opened, but He'll also close those doors that should be closed. Don't ask God to help make life easier. Ask Him to help make you better.

What we pray for is also very important. One of the worst disappointments to happen to you is when what you prayed for and believed God for doesn't turn out as expected. That's why we need to understand how God moves in response to our prayers. Praying is not a shot in the dark and not just about making requests, but it is the way we get connected and in position with the will of the Father.

Before I went bankrupt years ago, most of my prayers consisted of asking God to meet my needs. "Lord help me pay my bills. Oh God, make my children do well, help my marriage out. Lord take away these problems." You see God doesn't write checks to pay bills. We do! Neither does He train our children or make us treat our spouse right. The Bible provides the roadmap. The Holy Spirit will be our guide. But we are the ones behind the wheel of the car.

Now miracles do happen. Many of us are walking miracles and I see them all the time. but waiting for miracles is not an excuse for irresponsibility. You can't live your life chasing miracles without knowing that God also expects something from you.

When I was in debt, I was looking for the miracle man with a miracle check to make me miraculously debt free. I was praying for my kids to miraculously get A's in school. I was looking for God to miraculously make my wife realize that I am the king, the big kahuna, and what I say is law, no questions asked! I'm so glad I didn't hold my breath waiting for those miracles to come to pass. Now many things did come to pass (not the I am king, big kahuna, what I say is law part). They came through prayer, effort, focus, discipline, learning to make right decisions and God's faithfulness.

After I went bankrupt I began to ask God to not just meet my needs but to give me my heart's desire. *"Lord, I ask for abundance in my marriage and my finances so that we can give of ourselves as you lead. Even if that means making personal sacrifices so that others can be blessed. I pray that my children would excel in life and their love of You. Help me to be a godly example. Lord, give me the wisdom I need to make wise decisions to work through my problems. Make me a man of God as I build your kingdom around the world, through music, through business, through my life testimony, through whatever I put my hands to do."*

Praying from the heart which is where your true emotions live and not from the head. Head prayers are prayers that you think will impress people and will show God how knowledgeable you are. God owns it all. He's the master creator, not limited by time and human boundaries. He's kind of hard to impress! But of all the things in the universe that the Father has created for His pleasure, the one thing He wants more than all of that is your heart. Only through prayer, can you give that to Him. And don't be concerned about telling God what's really in your heart, even if it's not pretty. He won't be put off. He can handle it and steer you in the right path.

More than 60 percent of the Psalms are David crying out to God for one thing or another. Yet with all his wrangling with God, He was still considered a man after God's own heart.

Get your power back!

Recognize this; you have the same power from God working through you that brought Jesus from the dead. (Ephesians 1:18-20) The sooner you can accept that, the sooner you start to live your life with spiritual authority. It would be ridiculous to get up in the morning, dress yourself, start your car and then go hop into the back seat (unless you have a chauffeur). But that's how so many of us live our lives.

If you're in an abusive relationship, you don't have to wait for a sign from heaven to tell you to get out of harms way. The full force of heaven will guide you, but you can't wait for the abuser to tell you when it's time to leave.

We should all aspire to lead. It doesn't matter if you never lead a Fortune 500 corporation or an international ministry, but you need to learn to lead you! Lead yourself to a better career or business. Lead yourself out of destructive and needy relationships. Lead yourself out of unproductive busyness and commitments that don't fulfill you. Lead yourself out of being everybody's counselor and banker, and shoulder to cry on. You may very well be hindering somebody from getting his or her own power back by being his or her artificial power source. It's time to release some people into their destiny.

This may sound selfish and it is. God said, "love your neighbor as yourself." When you exhaust yourself and burden yourself with the weight of everyone's problems, you do not love yourself. Take charge of your life and let God do His job in the lives of other people. You make the decision with God's lead on what is important in your life and what is not. Stop giving your power away to people, to unhealthy habits and emotions. Stop seeing yourself as powerless. God sees you as more than a conqueror. God's power is not confined to the heavenlies. God's power is in you!

Get your joy back!

Unresolved and unrepentant sin can steal your joy. (See Psalm 51:8) What you constantly feed your mind can also steal your joy. I used to watch the news on TV first thing in the morning, listen to the news and talk radio in my car while driving. I'd watch the news late at night before going to bed. I'd hear about war, terrorism, child abuse, murder and all kinds of political wrangling. I would hear the same bad stories dissected and rehashed over and over again. No wonder I was filled with anxiety, biting my nails way down, and eating a lot of junk food!

There really is a lot of good that is going on in our world. There are people getting off of drugs everyday. Families are still being restored. Abuse victims are speaking out. Criminals are being prosecuted. Advances are being made in science and medicine. Things aren't perfect and this is certainly not a Utopian society. But I believe it's too one-sided in favor of bad news. But I guess good news doesn't sell. Good news won't get TV ratings. (Though I beg to differ!)

So I still listen to the news, but not all the time. I spend my day whether in the office, at home, in my car or on a plane singing and listening to things that bring me pleasure. In my iPod, I've got everything from Kirk Franklin to The Stylistics. (You know...the Stylistics...Betcha bye golly wow!) I also listen to conferences on CD. Not just preaching conferences but marketing and business. Writing conferences and motivational conferences. I love reading books and stories about people who survived horrendous situations. I have photos of my family on my computer and cell phone that I glance at throughout the day. Go ahead and listen and do things you enjoy.

But the absolute best thing to do is for you to get into the presence of the Lord. This is so much more than just the realization of the existence of God present throughout the world. I'm talking about opening a channel for the presence of God to become an integral part of your world. This is where you know that God knows you and hears you and feels you. I sing songs to Him and about Him. I'm learning to meditate and think on things that are pure, lovely and admirable. Things that are excellent and worthy of praise. (Philippians 4:7,8)

Sometimes I have to remind myself to think this way. It's so easy to let the feelings of fear and being overwhelmed come in. I remind myself that God is on my side, and with Him it really is more than if the whole world was against me. (Hope I don't ever have to face that!)

Get your worship back!

Jesus had friends and family, but He also made a few enemies. His preaching was seen as confrontational to the religious people of His day. He challenged their argumentative questions with answers that revealed their veiled hypocrisy. He healed on the Sabbath and was a friend of sinners. He made no apologies for who He was–the Son of the true and living God.

So much of our church worship has shrunk to "Diet Jesus" or "Jesus Light." Mediocre entertainment with a dash of refried preaching or a teaching series that my head already knows but still leaves my spirit empty. Maybe that's the new way of worship. I'm not referring to a particular style of worship here either. Whether you go to a church or meet with a few friends at home, worship needs to be more than an enthusiastic worship leader and a three point sermon. We need to worship and love God with all of our hearts, mind, soul and strength. I want something in my worship experience in church that I can't find on the Internet. I can't find it by just attending any old show.

Don't get me wrong. Some of my best times of worship are when I'm alone. I can read something on the Internet or even go to a movie and find something that is significant or spiritually impacting. But the fellowship with other people of faith and a fresh encounter with God can never be replaced by just studying about Him. I love when we join our hearts and our voices in unhindered praise to God.

A couple of years ago, my wife started a women's prayer meeting in our home. What started with three ladies has now grown to as many as 120 women meeting from all races and denominations once a month. No guys allowed! I could be lounging around watching television in the back bedroom, but when I hear those women unite their voices in song and prayer, it sets me on fire! Priceless!!

Don't get too comfortable!

I've been guilty of trying to take God out of heaven and putting Him in my comfort zone. If you've lost your sense of awe concerning the things of God, where the glory of God doesn't reside in your comfort zone. Don't just join a church– join the kingdom!

I love going to the theater. I love going to restaurants. I love hanging with loved ones. (I tolerate shopping). God's kingdom is so much more than just the mundane thing we call life. It is a supernatural encounter with the Spirit of God.

"For the kingdom of God is not a matter of eating and drinking, but of righteousness, peace and joy in the Holy Spirit." (Romans 14:16) I believe it was Chuck Swindoll who said, *"When you're feeling lost, God's presence brings hope. When you're faith is weak, joy will strengthen it. When you're feeling anxious, thanksgiving will lift your anxiety."*

The apostle Paul said, *"What I'm getting at, friends, is that you should simply keep on doing what you've done from the beginning. When I was living among you, you lived in responsive obedience. Now*

49

that I'm separated from you, keep it up. Better yet, redouble your efforts. Be energetic in your life of salvation, reverent and sensitive before God. That energy is God's energy; energy deep within you, God Himself willing and working at what will give him the most pleasure. Do everything readily and cheerfully –no bickering, no second-guessing allowed! Go out into the world uncorrupted, a breath of fresh air in this squalid and polluted society. Provide people with a glimpse of good living and of the living God. Carry the light-giving Message into the night so I'll have good cause to be proud of you on the day that Christ returns. You'll be living proof that I didn't go through all this work for nothing." (Philippians 2:12-16)

Clean the filter!

Now hear this...Our minds are filled with images and experiences of the past. Such as, if you didn't have loving parents or faced ridicule or abuse when you were a child. All that "data" is stored in your mind. If you grew up hearing harsh legalistic preaching, or were made to feel that you were never good enough or "saved" enough, the filter in your mind might be clogged. One of the reasons some people with weight issues don't lose weight is because they don't have a healthy self-image or self-esteem. Emotional eaters think that if they just lose the weight, then they'll have self-esteem.

Well in order for an emotional eater to lose weight and keep it off, he or she must recognize their self-value before starting a diet. If not, they'll probably just fall off the wagon, or gain the weight all back after losing it as soon as a situation comes that rattles the emotions. Perhaps that's why the diet industry thrives. It simply might be because for some, it treats the symptom, but not the root of the problem.

Many married couples go to counseling and seminars for their marriages. I believe every couple should go to a marriage seminar such as Family Life Weekend to Remember. (You can visit their website at www.FamilyLife.org). They are invaluable for teaching couples the skills and the power of oneness in marriage.

I also believe that you should work on yourself harder than you work on your marriage. The result is a stronger marriage. We bring our clogged filters and baggage into our relationships. If we work on cleaning out all the self-defeating junk in our minds, we'll become less defensive, more patient and forgiving, and able to esteem others higher than ourselves without feeling they're getting the upper hand.

So you ask, what does this have to do with deepening my relationship with God? Everything! Because no matter how much truth you hear, if it is filtered through a mind that says, *not me*, you'll only scratch the surface in getting your power back.

You are more than a conqueror...Not me.
God loves you and has a great plan for you...Not me.
You can do all things through Christ...Not me.
You don't have to live with anger...Not me.
You can walk through your fears...Not me.

Your past is not an indication of your future...Not me.
I think he really loves you...Not me.
You can get fit and healthy...Not me.

Would you say this prayer right now?
"Father, help me to see myself in the pages of this book. My heart is open. My spirit is open. I pray that You will help me confront the issues of my past and restore love and laughter as I yield to the power of Your Spirit. I pray that healing and wholeness would begin to come forth in my life at this very moment. In Jesus Name, Amen."

The Faith Life!

Without faith it is impossible to please God. To deepen your relationship with God, you must have faith. The only question is...what is faith? Some think faith is based on some legalistic mental process. They think that if you don't get what you believe God for, you don't have enough faith. Others think that faith is only for the bold, the courageous and they believe that you truly can't be a person of faith until you conquer all of your intimidation and fears.

Hebrews 11:1 says, *"...that faith is the confident assurance that what we hope for is going to happen."* For a long time though, that scripture left me confused. You see a whole lot of things that I had faith for didn't happen. I believed God was going to heal my mother when she was ill. She died. I believed the house I had up for sale was going to be sold before the closing on the new one. It didn't. I paid two mortgages for eight months. (Talk about pressure...). I believed that my son would give his heart to God when he was a teenager. He didn't. And so on, and so on. There were times I didn't believe I had faith because emotionally I didn't feel strong and powerful enough in a crisis situation. As a matter of fact, sometimes I just felt outright confused and helpless.

If truth be told, we are all faced with our doubt and indecision and how it all relates to our faith in God. Many people in the Bible that we consider pillars of faith, had moments of doubt also. Abraham, John the Baptist, David and others faced times when they doubted. Even Jesus Himself, while being crucified on a cross, cried out to the Father, *"My God, my God why have you forsaken me?"*

Another important point to recognize is that all of the people in the eleventh chapter of Hebrews' "hall of faith," received God's approval because of their faith, yet none of them received all that God had promised; none of them. (Read Hebrews 11:39)

Now the 40th verse reveals some telling information that many times is overlooked in discussions about faith. It says *"For God had far better things in mind for us that would also benefit them, for they can't receive the prize at the end of the race until we finish the race."* The whole emphasis on receiving what we believe cannot be based only on the concerns of today. The race isn't over yet.

Furthermore, we are still growing in our faith. We are at different levels of spiritual maturity. That's why the body of Christ is so essential to each other. *"He is the one who gave these gifts to the church:*

the apostles, the prophets, the evangelists, and the pastors and teachers. (Ephesians 4:11)

Their responsibility is to equip God's people to do his work and build up the church, the body of Christ, until we come to such unity in our faith and knowledge of God's Son that we will be mature and full grown in the Lord, measuring up to the full stature of Christ. Then we will no longer be like children, forever changing our minds about what we believe because someone has told us something different or because someone has cleverly lied to us and made the lie sound like the truth." (Hebrews 11:14)

To presume that just because we believe something to be will be, unless it has its foundation in the Word of God, is a set up for potential disappointment. So faith must join hands with prayer, with God's Word, and God's will. My premise is that I'm going to believe God for the impossible, while at the same time meditating and seeking to please Him. If I don't receive what I've prayed for, I am certain the Father knows what is best for me.

I love how the Amplified Bible puts it *"For I consider that the sufferings of this present time (this present life) are not worth being compared with the glory that is about to be revealed to us and in us and for us and conferred on us!"* (Romans 8:18)

What's astonishing to me is that many of the things I prayed for that didn't turn out as expected, eventually turned out "exceeding, abundantly" better than I had expected. I was asking for a base hit, and it's as though the Father hit a grand slam home run! For the expectations I've yet to see, He's given me peace and grace to stand. And that's more than enough for me.

So don't let your emotions get the best of you and watch out for the faith traps. The faith traps bring grave disappointment and even falling away from the faith when your prayer isn't answered.

Hype Driven Faith Trap
Declaring something because you want it to be, but it isn't. It has no Biblical basis. It is self-centered wishful thinking. God is not a partner in this. (John 15:6-7)

Double Minded Faith Trap
Not steady – chasing after teachings and revelations until you find something that feels good. Not really seeking for truth but agreement with your point of view to bring false comfort. (James 1:7)

Fragmented Faith Trap
Fragmented families – fragmented churches. There are people who constantly go at it alone. People who are willfully fragmented or separated off from other believers don't enjoy the full force of God's favor. (Matthew 18:19, 20) I believe the faith life can be summed up in Paul's words to Timothy. *"For God has not given us a spirit of fear and timidity, but of power, love, and a sound mind."* (2 Timothy 1:7)

Power – authority and boldness
Love – reaching out to others in caring and effective ministry
Sound Mind – self control, self discipline

So deepening our relationship with God is the journey of becoming transformed more and more into the image of Christ. Eliza Hewitt said it this way when she penned this timely hymn.

More about Jesus would I know,
More of His grace to others show;
More of His saving fullness see,
More of His love Who died for me.

More, more about Jesus,
More, more about Jesus;
More of His saving fullness see,
More of His love Who died for me.

More about Jesus let me learn,
More of His holy will discern;
Spirit of God, my teacher be,
Showing the things of Christ to me.

More about Jesus; in His Word,
Holding communion with my Lord;
Hearing His voice in every line,
Making each faithful saying mine.

More about Jesus; on His throne,
Riches in glory all His own;
More of His kingdom's sure increase;

More of His coming, Prince of Peace.

Chapter Three

DISCOVER YOUR PASSION (GETTING UNSTUCK)

Recently I read a story about James Polk, as he laid on his deathbed. Polk, who came from a privileged family, rose from being a lawyer to the Speaker of the House of Representatives to the eleventh President of the United States of America. Under Polk's administration the United States expanded by more than a million square miles. However, Polk's greatest weakness as President was not dealing with the growing issue of banning slavery.

With all of his accomplishments, the last words he spoke were to and about his wife Sarah. "I love you Sarah. For all eternity, I love you." By the way, he requested in his will that Sarah would free all of their slaves upon her death. I find that interesting. It seems he didn't have the courage to do in life, what he could do when death was knocking at the door.

Rich or poor, educated or illiterate, focused or clueless, at the final day of our lives, we don't have to look far to find our passions. Our true passions will find us.

And so I thought of my wife, my son and my daughters. I thought of my daughter-in-law and my grandbabies. I remembered the love of music when it wasn't how I earned a living. I remember the first time I was paid $75.00 to sing at a church in the South Bronx. I thought of when I had lost it all and I never thought that I'd find my way again. But by God's grace, I landed on my feet and what could have destroyed me only made me stronger. And I remembered the day when I finally got it. I could honestly look in the mirror and see that I am more than my job or what negative people may say about me or even my own self-defeating thoughts.

I am more than a conqueror and I am a child of God; fearfully and wonderfully made. I determined that as long as I have breath, that my passion would never get lost behind my work. Many fathers work hard to provide for their families, but then somewhere down the road, the work takes over the passion. Now he works to buy a bigger house or car. He works to escape the problems of life or because of the ego satisfaction he receives from his position. When this takes over, the very family he is providing for becomes secondary to his career, his ego, or his ministry.

Balance? I'm not exactly sure what that is. I do know that the right passions of your life will keep bringing you back to the right purposes. But why wait until you're ready to check out before breaking away from the pack and start doing what your heart tells you to do.

After graduating from high school, I didn't

attend college. I planned to but since I was already working as an assistant manager in the shoe department at the local mall, I figured I was one step away from the "big time" shoe department manager.

I would soon find out that all of my hopes and dreams would later be dashed by reality. I was on a head on collision with a rude awakening that would make me look at the world in a different way.

I was confronted with the reality of whether I trusted God enough to answer my prayers anymore. I know I didn't value my own decisions anymore. You see, I had made one too many bad decisions; one too many disappointments. My passions were still there. They were just hidden under many layers of low self-esteem and people pleasing.

You see by the time I reached the age of thirty-four I had worked at over sixteen different jobs. I had been bankrupt twice, evicted from two apartments, on public assistance, and our home had been foreclosed. All this happened to me with a wife and three children.

I'll never forget the day I walked out of bankruptcy court for what would be the last time. Just an hour earlier, I sat motionlessly in the last row wondering how in the world did things get this bad. Where am I going to move with my family? What in the world am I going to do with my life now? My credit is shot. My job prospects slim. Furthermore, I'm not even sure I have the will to try again. Dear God, I'm not sure things could get much worse than this. And then it did.

While I was waiting for my case to be called, most of the time my eyes were glued looking down at my feet. As I happened to glance up, I noticed a man in front of me looking straight at me. "Hey, aren't you Alvin Slaughter? I love your music!" My cover was blown. "Yes I am," as my last ounce of self-esteem hit the floor. "I guess it happens to the best of us," says my "admirer" turning his head forward.

My case is finally called. Some legal rambling by the judge, and then I'm declared...bankrupt. Not the worst thing to ever happen in the world; just the worst thing to happen in my world.

As I turned to leave the court, a newly declared bankrupt, I felt like a big "L" for loser had been stamped on my forehead. I opened the door and walked into the corridor and to my surprise, the most unexpected thing happened.

A wave of peace washed over me as though I had just won the lottery. I was prepared to spend the rest of the day wallowing in my self-pity, and questioning whether prayer was really worth the effort and expectation. But I believe God had sent His ministering angels to prop up my shoulders, and lift up my head. I was immediately reminded of the great quote by author Corrie Ten Boom. "There is no pit so deep, that God's love is not deeper still."

The Bible says that God gives beauty for ashes, the garment of praise for the spirit of heaviness. (Isaiah 61:3) Somewhere deep in my soul, right then and there, God revived a new passion in me to take his message of love and empowerment to the world. I had no idea how this was going to happen.

I just knew that something supernatural was shaping my life.

Since I was twelve years old, I had been a thousand percent involved in church and gospel music. (Except for a stint when I left because I thought church was irrelevant.)

As a young married man, I worked six days a week in the mall or at shoe stores which required long hours. Later on, I spent years working in sales and commission only jobs, so that I could make my own hours. Gospel music was literally my life. It's where I found my greatest satisfaction and sense of accomplishment. I wanted to be available in case I was needed at church or to rehearse and sing in various choirs and small groups. I didn't want to miss a thing.

I loved singing and watching the faces of the congregation, as I would sing songs about God's love and power. It was a natural high for me to see grand mamas crying and young mamas dancing as I sang my songs of praise. There was one small problem. I was a horrible salesman and made very little money. I don't even have to tell you the strain this caused on my family. Yes, I had faith, but not much wisdom.

So my passion was always there. It eventually just got crushed under the weight of life. Depression and stress are passion stealers. I didn't think that I could ever sing professionally, so I never pursued music as a profession until much later in life. Truth is, I wasn't really sure what I could do. You see this chapter is not about asking you, if you have a passion in life? I've written this chapter to tell you that you do.

Microsoft founder and billionaire Bill Gates has a passion of bringing innovations in health and learning to the global community through the Bill and Melinda Gates Foundation. (www.gatesfoundation.org)

Lisa Beamer, whose husband Todd died on United Airlines Flight 93 on 9/11 founded The Todd M. Beamer Foundation. Heroic Choices, as the foundation is now called, is a non-profit, youth services organization that helps children who have experienced trauma. (www.heroicchoices.org)

I met a woman at an event in Rome, Georgia some years ago. As I greeted her and we began to talk, I learned that her vocation was being a schoolteacher. But her passion was traveling the world teaching and caring for children in developing nations. As I looked at the vest she was wearing, she had patches that represented the different countries she had visited over the years. It was amazing to see the sparkle in her eyes as she identified the country and service that she had given to that area. The passion was burning for teaching and aiding impoverished and orphaned children who had run out of options. You see she had incorporated her vocation into her passion. By the way, you don't have to start your own organization. You can join with one that shares the same passion you have.

And then there are the passions that are just plain fun. Marketing guru Dan Kennedy has made millions showing businesses strategies to grow their businesses but his passion is racing his horses. (www.dankennedy.com) Some take dance classes, some write poetry, and I love to ride motorcycles. (Sometimes really fast!)

One of the most valuable things I have learned over the years about the discovery of passion is that passions can change. As a matter of fact, they often do, simply because people change. I used to beat myself over the head because I could not understand why the thing that made me tick years ago didn't anymore. It was nothing to panic about or to start seeing a psychiatrist over. I had changed and therefore my passions had as well.

The same woman who traveled to third world countries to teach, later adopted a young child, I believe from Africa, whose face had been disfigured as a result of an accident. Now her passion is caring for the child and raising money to have plastic surgery performed on this child so that she can regain the face that was lost in such a terrible way. (I wish I knew more about her so that I could give contact information.) Can you see how her passions evolved as her life changed? Your purpose can evolve into many things.

You will truly know your passion when you feel God's favor while you're doing it. There is this guiding focus that fills you when you are living in your passion. That doesn't necessarily mean that you're going to become the next American Idol because you love to sing. Sometimes we have to accept our passion for what it is. It may not lead to a career opportunity but may be something that brings

a sense of worth and fulfillment. It helps you discon-
nect from the pressures of life.

I love riding motorcycles. I literally feel God's
presence when I ride. It helps me to relax and think
clearer. Some love fine art, while others love to cook.
Don't think your passion must be an earth shaking
passion – it could be that you are a great listener, or
great server, singer or writer. It does not really matter what the passion is by name or function. What is
most important is that whatever your passion is, your
heart is there also. The satisfaction that you get from
connecting with your passion brings you a greater
sense of well-being emotionally. And this will affect
the quality of your life and of those around you.

My long time office manager, Ruth is a wonderful woman who along with her husband, raised
three brilliant children. They're either in graduate
school, or working successfully in corporate jobs.
With all the kids gone, the nest is empty and now is
the time to kick back into some "us" time. Well, Ruth's
husband thought it would be a great idea to get a
dog. A dog! Ruth wasn't necessarily jumping up and
down at the idea because she had a hunch that eventually she would be doing the feeding and walking
and cleaning up after poochie. She eventually gave
in because a dog would sort of force them to get
outside and do a little more exercising.

Not too many days passed when Barney finally arrives to his new home from the animal shel-
ter. A cute little mixed breed that anyone could love.
Only one problem–Barney had apparently suffered

so much physical abuse by his previous owner that he constantly shook with fear.

After months of caring for this frightened little dog, Barney began to slowly trust people again. He never, ever barked and was in heaven when you'd rub his head. The more hands rubbing, the better! Not exactly Fido the guard dog, but he has a face that could even bring a non-dog lover to his knees.

Well, because of his loving, gentle nature and after months of school and advanced training, Barney is now a certified therapy dog. Ruth and Barney visit cancer patients, and other people with life threatening diseases and their families, at a major hospital in Pennsylvania.

It seems like Barney has found his passion. But this story is really about Ruth. Her eyes well up with tears when she tells the stories of how this little, formerly abused and abandoned dog brings so much joy to people ravaged by the process of chemotherapy and disability. He's also a welcome distraction to their families lingering nearby for hours in the hospital waiting room.

I'm so sure that Ruth gets immense joy and euphoria working at Alvin Slaughter International! (Hey, that's a joke...) But how could she have ever known that deciding to get a dog, and an abused one at that, would help be the source of her passion to reach out to people in her own personal way.

There is so much going on in our minds and our lives that sometimes we get depressed when we feel we have no passions. Listen, I believe we need to learn to live and connect with the spirit of the moment. When we are told what time to go to work, and when we can take a lunch break, and how much money we can earn, we eventually don't even know how to connect with our spirit. We'll cover that in another chapter, but know this...RELAX. You don't have to find your passion today. Live in the Spirit. Your passion will find you. The most important thing is to watch out for passion stealers! These are things that rob you of peace and connecting with the Spirit of God.

• Don't let anyone suck the life out of you!

It's okay to be a good listener and offer help when you can, but sometimes you're just one telephone call away from someone nagging and complaining about someone or something. When someone just wants to unload all their stuff on you, but they're not really interested in your opinion or advice, cut the conversation short and use caller ID.

Also, I never understand when people always moan about how busy they are. Learn how to say "NO" and stop trying to be all things to all people. When you can't say 'NO' to people, and you've allowed them to stress you out, you're probably prideful. You're too concerned with what people think of you. You've got to find your grounding in you and not the opinions of others. If someone rails and complains to me about how I don't return calls or they spend more time than I'm comfortable with chatting about nothing, I put them on my "goodbye list." Life brings enough pressure. Why take on more? You need to create a life where you can breathe, without people sucking the life out of you.

• Reach out - Open your eyes, your ears, and your heart.

Some years ago, when I was invited to sing in Africa, it gave me a love and a passion for the people of that great continent. Life is surrounded by opportunities where just your simplest act of compassion will change someone else's world in a big way. When you reach out to someone where there is a genuine need, it will always connect your spirit with God's Spirit.

Oh, the joys of those who are kind to the poor. The LORD rescues them in times of trouble.

The LORD protects them and keeps them alive. He gives them prosperity and rescues them from their enemies.

The LORD nurses them when they are sick and eases their pain and discomfort. (Psalm 41:1-3)

Reaching out to others who are in need is a spiritual principal. It takes your eyes off of yourself as being the center of the universe, which leads to pride. Remember, Lucifer's fall from heaven wasn't because of sexual immorality or stealing money. It was because of pride.

• Don't hide.

Running away from problems usually just makes them worse. Learn to tackle hard projects at the start of the day so that you won't spend the rest of the day avoiding them. Avoiding problems compounds them and you waste time stressing instead

67

of problem solving. Solutions will come as situations are dealt with. Human nature sometimes seeks the path of least resistance, but you're going to have to face the problem eventually. So face the giant now, get it over with, and free your mind up.

Procrastinators live in this false state of busy-ness. If you're busy and accomplishing little, you are only fooling yourself! Write down your objectives and then put them on a timetable. You will develop the habit of getting a lot done, and not feeling constantly overwhelmed.

• What prayer will and will not do.

When we pray, we can recognize the reality of God's presence. Prayer empowers us to be still and know God – finding guidance in every circum-stance. Prayer is also the channel where we submit to the Father in reverence and humility. It is also the pipeline where we receive the strength of the Lord.

"If you need wisdom – if you want to know what God wants you to do – ask Him, and He will gladly tell you. He will not resent your asking. But when you ask him, be sure that you really expect Him to an-swer, for a doubtful mind is as unsettled as a wave of the sea that is driven and tossed by the wind.

People like that should not expect to receive any-thing from the Lord. They can't make up their minds. They waver back and forth in everything they do." (James 1:5-8)

So after you pray, you've got to do. Take steps in faith. They don't have to be huge steps. I'm not saying you should throw caution to the wind. I'm also not saying you should pray once then off you go. What I am saying is to continue to seek the Lord and to continue praying as you go. Fear just laughs in the face of your prayers if you don't act. Too many people call themselves waiting on God when in fact God is waiting on them. Remember, faith without works is dead. (James 2:20)

• Don't go numb, pain acknowledges that you've been hurt.

My wife and I have a dear friend who has quietly endured so much physical and emotional abuse over the years. When she eventually shared what she had been through over her lifetime, there were no tears. It was as though she was numb and resigned to the way life was. She lost her passion for life and had had too many broken promises. Too many unfulfilled dreams. Why even care anymore. The less she cares, the less she can be hurt again.

Chest pains might indicate a heart attack. A toothache may lead to a pulled tooth or root canal. No one wants to feel pain. But pain is an indication that something is wrong and should cause you to acknowledge that you don't want to feel this way.

So when you hurt don't be afraid to cry for help. You will never change what you don't acknowledge. And cry as loud and as often as you need to until the healing begins. I believe everyone should be connected with a Christ centered, Bible believing, loving and worshipping church. For in this right kind of environment, there is healing. But if you are in a controlling, judgemental, legalistic church, run like the wind!

• Don't wait for anybody to make your life for you, make your own life!

I am constantly meeting people who are upset or discouraged because they can't find anyone to help them start their new business, support their new ministry, or buy into their ideas. Look, when you start living with passion, don't expect a parade to start following you down the street. You need to prove yourself to yourself first. People are drawn to leaders. Leaders solve problems. Leaders inspire. Leaders find a way when the average can't see a way. Get a backbone. Whiners aren't leaders. There is an old saying that goes like this. Lead...follow...or get out of the way!

• Seek peace and healing for your life.

Get away from toxic people and toxic thoughts. Toxic people are pride-filled, self-centered careless people who only see the weaknesses and shortcomings of others, but never, ever their own. Sometimes you can't totally avoid people like this, but never ever allow people like this to rule your head or your heart. Sometimes you've got to put people in their place. I know this is uncomfortable for some, but we're grown folk now. Being an adult means that I'm responsible for all my mistakes. But I'm also responsible for my sanity! Not only should we find peace and healing in our lives, but every chance we get, we should give peace and healing away to someone else. Oh, by the way, make sure you're not a toxic person yourself!

70

Chapter Four
NEXT LEVEL BELIEF!

This was the biggest concert I had ever personally done. I was told that more than 50,000 people filled the stadium and there were more than that outside who couldn't get in. The Nelson Mandela Stadium in Namboole, Uganda was packed with people soaked from the pouring rain who had pressed their way to get to this one night worship experience.

I had the privilege of meeting the first lady of Uganda, who along with her security and entourage had come to share in this monumental event. An African choir made up of hundreds of voices enthusiastically sang as the masses of people moved to the beat. Our host for the event, Pastor Kayanja, eventually took the stage and after greetings, began to share his heart about how important this event was to his nation.

Uganda made headlines back in the seventies and early eighties because of their notorious dictator Idi Amin. It was common to read in the headlines about the brutality and murder that he ordered on thousands of his own people. When my generation thinks of this African nation, unfortunately horrible thoughts of murder and mayhem come to mind.

Although Idi Amin is no longer in power, to-day it is still a long hard road of building their infra-structure and economy to secure the future of the beautiful people of Uganda. Diseases, witchcraft, poverty, and terrorism are just some of the battles that are raging in their land.

Prior to my introduction, Pastor Kayanja spoke to the thousands of people. I felt this very uneasy feeling in the pit of my stomach. Although I had sung on many of the great stages around the world at times with some of the greatest speakers and evangelists, I felt woefully inadequate.

You see to me, I was just a singer. Not a preacher. No healing ministry to speak of. No feed-ing program. I'm not a medical missionary or a per-son of influence in the political arena. I didn't have millions of dollars at my disposal to build schools or hospitals. I was just...a singer.

I don't write books. I don't make waves. I'm just a singer of songs. No platinum CD sales or Grammy awards. I'm not a household name. I sing a few songs, say a few words of encouragement and then I go back home. Home where the food is always good, the bed is nice and warm and wel-coming and the remote control is never far away, at home in my comfort zone. That's what I did and I thought that was all I'd ever do. At least that's what I believed.

Well God was faithful that evening. He met us in a powerful and supernatural way. People were spiritually hungry and God will always meet you at the point of your need when you call out to him in faith. Perhaps it was the faith of the people that ushered in God's presence. Maybe God would've blessed us anyway, in spite of our faith. All I know is on that night, it seemed as though my belief in my ability to make a difference had taken flight and left the arena. What could I sing or say that would leave a lasting impact on the lives of the people?

In my little moment of temporary insanity, I should have realized the power the spoken word has to speak death or life into someone's future. I forgot that I was singing about something that I had been deeply committed to all of my life. I had believed the Gospel was the power of God unto salvation. Somehow I missed that the Gospel message is so much more than just jumping and shouting and "having church." It's a message of love and empowerment, having a renewed mind and focus. It's a message of hope that goes way beyond temporary things and ascends to higher realms of things eternal. The message is about the power of Jesus' name and not about me.

I should have realized that my belief is based on the principles and promises of God, whether I feel it, can physically see it or not. To be grounded in my belief in God and what He called me to do, not just my experiences. At the time, I was so focused on my perceived inadequacies; I just didn't see it that way.

Some people can never see themselves as happy complete individuals. Some people repeatedly find themselves in unhealthy relationships because they can't see themselves with someone who truly cares about them and treats them with respect and dignity. Others can never see themselves as intelligent and independent, so they're always looking to someone else to make the tough calls for their own life. While still some see everything negatively, instead of realizing as Napoleon Hill once said, "In every adversity lies the seed of equal or greater opportunity." Your life, in the long run, reflects how you see yourself, whether good or bad.

Years ago, I remember talking to a good friend of mine who was a musician. Times were not going well and he and his family were struggling financially. I told him how I used to drive a taxicab for a few months, years ago, to earn extra income. (I hated that job! No offense to cab drivers.) I used to sell burglar alarms, life insurance, panty hose (yes panty hose!), magazine subscriptions, carpet and a long list of other stuff to supplement my passion of singing Christian music. I also told him that even now, although successful as a singer/songwriter, I was building side businesses unrelated to music.

"Well I went to college for music, I'm not driving a cab or anything else!" he says. "I can't see myself doing anything but music." I understand. Point taken. He only saw himself as a musician. The only problem was that he was also a husband, father, rent payer, auto loan payer, kid's school supplies purchaser, grocery store shopper, clothes wearer, yada, yada, yada—you get the picture.

I understand. I'm just not sure the wife, the kids, the landlord, the finance company, and Wal-Mart understands. Although bank robbery can be lucrative, the consequences are, let's just say, less than favorable. You are more than your past. You are more than your education, your job title and salary.

One-dimensional people hinder true creativity at best and lack problem-solving skills at worst. The creation of solutions to problems is endless when you tap into next level belief.

Now I know that you may be facing an extraordinary event that doesn't happen everyday. That's the very reason you need 'next level belief'. You see part of next level belief is to visualize who, what and where you want to be. This is more than just daydreaming. Daydreaming is to think about something without a plan in place to ever make it happen. When you rehearse this in your mind over and over, with a plan in place, you're not unprepared when you finally reach the door to what you've believed for...that's 'next level belief'.

The plan of a wise parent is to love, discipline and educate their child because as much as we love them, one day our children must learn figuratively and literally to walk on their own two feet. We all try to keep our babies little and cuddly as long as possible, but a thirty-five year old baby isn't cute. It is so important that we see and affirm the potential in our children. That's why we who are parents and grandparents need to say to our children "Yes Johnny, you could be a fireman. Mary you could be a doctor."

When my son was two, I saw him as a baby. When he was sixteen, I saw him as a teenager. Now that he's an adult I see and respect him as a man, husband and father. Since he was my oldest, it was hard seeing him grow from a boy to a man. Letting go was one of the hardest things for me to do. If I hadn't eventually seen him as a man, I'd probably be meddling in his life and treating him like he was a kid.

Jesus asked Peter, *"Who do you say I am?"* Peter could have responded a teacher or prophet. But he said, *"You are the Christ, the son of the living God."* (Matthew 16:17) Peter gave the right answer because he saw Jesus the right way. Since he saw Jesus the right way, he received a promotion and later became the keynote speaker on the day of Pentecost.

So the first step to 'next level belief' is that you must visualize it. Not with your eyes. See it in your mind. Feel it in your heart. Receive it in your spirit.

I believe the biggest battle we face in our world today is psychological warfare. Media, religion, big business, and sports–it seems everyone is fighting for a chunk of our psychological real estate. How we think of ourselves, how we think of others and whether we choose to act or not to act on what we believe will determine the course of our families, our nation, our world, and ourselves.

I once heard a Pastor from Ghana say that Africans pray more than any other nation on the earth, yet they are one of the poorest. Prayer doesn't change you. What you believe changes you. If you line up your prayer with what you believe, you access the power to create change.

When you go through a divorce, financial failure, or you've just blown it, your biggest problem may not be your lack of belief in God. It could be that you no longer believe in yourself. You see yourself as a loser and a failure.

You are held captive or set free by what you believe. You'll never change your life until you change what you believe and do. The major difference between where you are today and where you were the same time last year is what you have believed.

Albert Einstein was not a religious man in a conventional sense, but I'm convinced that Einstein, one of the most intelligent humans that has ever lived, was no fool either. He once said that the significant problems we face couldn't be solved at the same level we were at when we created them. 'Next level belief' is a new way of thinking resulting in a new way of doing, resulting in a new way of being.

We were not designed be get stuck in a defeated mindset. Nor should we be comfortable not challenging who and what we believe. God never expected us to enter the church building and check our brains at the door. He won't get nervous. God accepts the challenge. Your doubts should ultimately bring you to a place of decision, which will only solidify what you believe.

If you seek me you will find me
When you seek me with all of your heart.
(Jeremiah 29:13)

When you truly find out who God is, you find out who you are. And He has a lot to say about you. You are the beloved of God, fearfully and wonderfully made. You are a generation chosen to make known the purpose, power and presence of God. And the confidence we have, is that He didn't leave us here to fend for ourselves. He sent His Spirit.

You don't have to face life alone. The Spirit empowers you. As a matter of fact, the same immeasurable power that raised Jesus from the dead is the same immeasurable Spirit power that lives inside of you.

The second step to 'next level belief' is to confirm it in your spirit. Which is your human spirit joining with God's Holy Spirit. It is God's will becoming your will.

I love reading the comments that people enter on my website at **www.alvinslaughter.com** The comments come from people who has either seen me on the Trinity Broadcasting Network or heard one of my CDs or attended one of my concerts. They encourage me when I'm a little weary. They remind me that I can still be effective when I feel I've blown it. Please allow me to share some of these personal gems with you.

"The music I have listened to from Alvin Slaughter has truly ministered to me and blessed me. When I was listening to "God Can Do Anything" last year in October, I was involved in a roll over automobile accident. I walked away without any injuries and my car was totaled. That song has become my theme song and I preach/teach it everywhere I go."

D. Woods

"I just want to tell you how much I am enjoying your new CD (The Faith Life). This is the most beautiful, uplifting and inspirational album that I've heard in a long time. It touches my heart very deeply. There's one song in particular (Worshippers) that makes me feel as if GOD is in my presence. What a joyous feeling. I find myself reaching out to the world spreading LOVE to everyone in need and praying that they are feeling what I'm feeling. PRAISE GOD!! Keep doing the good work and reaching out to the world. Hope to see you in my town soon."

V. Venable

"What can I say, except, Thank you! I knew I was supposed to contact you for this interview and was grateful when the request was accepted. But I had no idea the amount of ministry and encouragement that would come from someone I have so much admiration, gratitude and respect for.

Thank you for your gracious, humorous and sincerely powerful spirit. It was a major blessing with all the focus on Christian breakups and divorces that I could see and hear the voice of a man that loves, respects and honors his wife. I could go on and on.... but I wanted you to know how grateful I am to such a wonderful God that would speak through his vessel to prompt me to continue in this way and walk there in."

D. Lockett

"Wow I have always been a great follower of your music. I've always clinged to the song " Holy, Holy, Holy" I thank God for your inspirational life. I used to be so ashamed to sing in front of people, as I was shy, etc., But once I watched your videos it gave me inspiration and from then I wanted to express my love for God without any hinderance. Thank you Alvin. God Bless you and your ministry."

M. Vakacavu

I am certainly not trying to show off or impress anyone with these comments. I just want you to see that there was a time in my life when I never believed I had what it took to effectively be used by God to bless somebody's life. Even when He was using me, I didn't believe He was.

When I finally realized that God was using me, I never believed that I could impact anyone besides my local church family. My mind kept expanding, and eventually I started believing for what to me seemed impossible, but I knew with God everything is possible.

After singing in choirs for years, and working as everything from a shoe salesman to a burglar alarm salesman, the time was right. I left my job, stepped down from the choir and launched out into full-time music ministry. That was over sixteen years ago. Who would have thought that now after all these years, I would have traveled all over the world singing and speaking about the love, the joy and the power of God.

This would not have happened if I visualized it, said yes to the Spirit but took no steps toward what I believed was my life's mission.

So the third step to 'next level belief' is to create it with your actions. Take small steps or big steps. It doesn't matter, just get moving and begin creating momentum.

My Ugandan experience was the impetus for my 'next level belief'. My 'next level belief' is to build the kingdom of God, inspire others to build the kingdom of God and to make Jesus famous. I'm connected with a ministry in Africa to train up leaders to stem the tide of poverty and disease in their own nation.

I'm not here to fit industry standards. I'm not here to blend in, but I am here to be a blessing. I'm a grown man and I'm my own man. I'm not looking for anyone's approval but the Father's, to love, as He would have me to love in the way He would have me do it.

What about you? I want you to know that there will be times when your belief is strong. And there will also be other times, you may not believe enough. If this happens, go back to Chapter 2, Deepening

Your Relationship With God. Get started today on your personal journey of next level belief. On the following pages, write down what you are believing for. Put it in a place where you can see it—pray on it—act on it—become it.

1. **Visualize it**—What is your goal? Write down how or where you see yourself 12 months from now.

2. **Confirm it in your spirit**—Write down what commitments you are going to do everyday to feed your spirit and connect with God.

3. **Create it with your actions**—What is your plan and what steps are you going to take. As you write it down, be specific and put a timetable on when you are going to take these actions.

(additional note pages in the back of the book)

I Believe by Alvin Slaughter

To know God is to love God
To love God is to serve God
To serve God is to believe in God

We must believe until the weary citizens of this generation find rest and peace for their soul

Believe until the broken hearted find a balm for healing and forgiveness

Believe until the evil of prejudice is an ancient thing of our ignorant past

Believe until every wide eyed, tender hearted little boy and little girl really, really knows that, "yes Jesus loves me"

Believe so that the cleansing blood of Christ will never be in vain

Believe until somebody...whosoever will...anybody can see the love of God in you and in me

Believe...and keep on believing

Believe until the whole wide world knows that yes, there is a more excellent way

And now abides faith, hope and love.... these three.

But the greatest of these.............is love.

Chapter Five
GET Going!

I thought about writing this book for years. As a matter of fact a publisher approached me a few years ago to discuss the prospects of writing a book, but I felt I had nothing to say.

I had been scratching my thoughts, ideas and experiences on pieces of paper, on my laptop and PDA for many, many years. But I didn't take the time to develop them or do anything with them.

Once I was having lunch with a Pastor friend of mine who was in the middle of writing another book. As an author, he understood the process, patience and discipline required to write a book. I commented to him that I could never write a book. He asked me why. I replied something to the effect that I can't. It's just not my thing.

Pastor David said something that gave me a rude awakening. He said how sad it was that I've had the experiences of a lifetime traveling the world, experiencing different cultures, life changing encounters, meeting interesting and important people, to just end up scratching what I've learned and experienced on little scrap pieces paper. No one will ever benefit from these experiences. When I'm long gone, my thoughts will go to the grave and my papers will be lost in a box in the attic or thrown out with the trash.

Of course writing isn't for everyone. But Pastor David saw right through my lame excuse and nailed the real issue right on the head. He said that my problem was not that I couldn't write—but that I would not discipline myself to write. I was focusing too much on whether all the effort involved would end up being a bestseller, rather than leaving a legacy; an inheritance of wisdom to my children and to my grandchildren. This is irresponsible at best and is certainly not being a good steward of the blessings that God has given to me. Now that was a wake up call! So the next time an opportunity came around, I jumped on it.

Here I am a few years later, creating my first book on what life has taught me through the years. And you know, I ended up really enjoying the process. As I began to write, I even started thinking about other topics and books that I want to write about after finishing this one. The funny thing is that I hated writing years ago when I was in school. I just wondered, how could I enjoy it now? I love to talk. I love to sing. I love to laugh, I love to eat and I love shows. And now thanks to my friend, Dee, who encouraged me in my writing, add to that—I love to write.

The interesting thing about getting started with anything is that on the journey to your desired goal, some of the pitfalls and interruptions along the way may in fact turn out to be blessings in disguise.

It's as though you're a passenger on a plane to Chicago. However, the plane is diverted to Philadelphia because of bad weather in Chicago. While stranded in Philly, you engage in a long conversation with a stranger who ends up eventually becoming a good friend, a business associate or maybe even your spouse.

Procrastinating will kill your future. Don't stop living while waiting for your miracle. God will bring miracles into your life according to His will. Get going and start living the faith life. Make this your year of living with focus and intention. The fear of what may or may not happen is natural.

The fact is that everything you hope for will not happen, but even at it's worst, God causes everything to work together for the good of those who love Him and are called according to his purpose.

Nine months after Jonathan White was married, a drunk driver ran a red light going 90 MPH and hit his parent's car. (For more info see www.jonathanwhitemusic.com) His father died instantly, and his mother lived for sixteen days in the hospital and then went on home to be with the Lord.

Jonathan and his wife thought they were entering a brighter phase of life when they found out that she was pregnant the year following his parents' accident. "We were so excited, because we were thinking that this would help heal the hurt that had been caused by losing my parents," said Jonathan. However, the doctors did not have good news for the Whites. Jonathan and Sheila were soon informed after their daughter's birth that the baby more than likely had Down Syndrome.

"I was angry, thinking that God had given us second best," said Jonathan. "However, I have found that God knows exactly what He is doing, and He gave us the very best that He had. Brittany has been a wonderful blessing to us and many others."

Years ago, songwriter Bruce Carroll recorded a song about a couple he knew who had a child born with Down's syndrome called, "Sometimes Miracles Hide." (www.brucecarroll.com)

They were so excited it was coming to be,
two people so in love and now soon there would
be three,
for many years they planned it.
Now soon it would be true,
She was picking out the pink clothes;
he was looking at the blue.

The call came unexpected the
doctor had bad news,
Some tests came back and things weren't right,
said you're gonna have to choose,
"I'll wait a week for your decision"
and then the words cut like a knife,
"I'm sure everyone will understand if you want to
end its life."

*Though they were badly shaken they
just had no choice,
Because they knew God creates no accidents and
they were sure they heard His voice sayin'.*

*(chorus)
Sometimes miracles hide,
and God will wrap some blessings in disguise
and you may have to wait this lifetime
to see the reasons with your eyes,
cause sometimes miracles hide*

*It seemed before they knew it the appointed day
arrived,
with eager apprehension they could barely hold inside,
The first time they laid eyes on her confirmed the
doctors fears
but they held onto God promise they were sure they
both could hear.*

*(chorus)
Sometimes miracles hide,
and God will wrap some blessings in disguise
and you may have to wait this lifetime
to see the reasons with your eyes,
cause sometimes miracles hide*

*Though she was not like the other girls they thought
she was the best,
and through all the years of struggle neither whis-
pered one regret.
And the first day that she started school and took
her first bus ride,*

*they'd remembered the words that God had spoke
and they both broke downand cried.*

*You see to them it did not matter why some things in
life take place,
cause they just knew the joy they felt when they'd
look into her face.*

*They learned that sometimes miracles hide,
they said God Has wrapped our blessing in disguise
and we may have to wait this lifetime to see the reasons with our eyes,
we know sometimes miracles hide. We've learned
sometimes miracles hide.*

Hidden behind the process of getting started is the seed of blessing and empowerment. Don't wait for the perfect time and situation to get started do-ing what's in your heart to do and becoming the per-son you want to be. Besides, what is perfect?

Even if you could snap your fingers and make the perfect life, it would end up flawed. Life could never be perfect without it's imperfections. What would we measure it up against? Once you get used to "perfection" and the newness starts to wear off, you start searching for a new version of perfection.

You are made in the image of the creator. And though we're not God, we have the power to create. We create through preparation and activity. God works on our behalf in His own time, opening every door that should be opened and closing every door that should be shut.

Preparation + activity + time = opportunity

This is not just about working hard to make a better life. This is about getting your power back by attracting true wealth into your life by the promises of God and by using what you have in your hand.

True wealth is so much more than big cars and big houses. True wealth is to have abundance in your life to give to others economically, socially and spiritually.

One of the greatest things I've had to learn is to get over myself and get to letting people know that we've got to move past this stuff that clogs our minds and move on to sharing the love of God.

Living paycheck to paycheck is a horrible way to exist. You're just one crisis away from losing everything. You have sleepless nights and constant fear that you'll be living on the streets.

A terrible pain to feel is the pain of a broken heart. A deep agonizing pain that reaches into the pit of your soul. You feel devastated...lost...powerless.

To say that you know God, but not being close enough to Him to get solutions and know the joy of serving Him is depressing.

This is all like spiritual and emotional quicksand! So whatever part of this book you've got to read again, do it, pray and meditate on it and then get started becoming the powerful person God made you to be.

5 WAYS TO KICK START YOUR PROCESS OF GETTING GOING

1. Anticipate victory

Failure is part of the process of life, but to have constant thoughts of failure is self-defeating. Sometimes we never get going because we don't feel we can succeed. Every endeavor of life has it's consequences but you will never win at getting your power back, until you convince yourself that it is possible for you.

2. Begin with the end in mind

Develop a blueprint for how you're going to get to the place in life you want to be. You don't need all the details, but you must become a visionary and not only a dreamer. Dreamers think about what they want to be. Visionaries develop strategies to help them get there. Most of the time you'll have to tweak your strategy because you will run into some roadblocks along the way. No problem. The more you strategize the better you become at it.

3. Become a student of personal development

Overcome fear, failure and people's opinion of you. Learn how to deal with rejection. Become a person of influence.

All of these things come by personal development. Some people call it self help or self discovery. Call it what you want, but your mind is the command center that will get you going.

One of the reasons people don't lose weight is because they don't have a healthy self-image or low self-esteem. That's why the diet industry thrives. It is because it treats the symptom and not the root of the problem.

People find themselves working on bad marriages. If they only work on their bad marriage and not on personally developing themselves individually, they will probably end up divorced.

When we work on ourselves, we become less defensive, more patient and understanding. We begin to let go of the baggage that we bring to our relationships.

If you don't read a lot, you can get books on CD, conference speakers on CD or DVD or actually attend an event geared towards developing your mind. Anything by Joyce Meyer, Stephen Covey, Joel Osteen, T.D. Jakes and this book you're reading right now will help get you on the right track. One of the greatest sources of personal development for me are the books of John, Ephesians and Romans in the Bible.

Personal development is an ongoing process in our lives so make it your mission and responsibility to continue to grow by being *"transformed by the renewing of your mind. Then you will be able to test and approve what God's will is—His good, pleasing and perfect will."* (Romans 12:2,3)

4. **Sell, sell, and sell!**

Let me dwell on this for a moment. Selling has had a bad rap over the years because of unscrupulous practices by pushy, unethical salespersons selling you stuff you really don't want or need. You must learn how to sell in order to get your power back. Selling in and of it self isn't bad. Nothing happens in life until a sale is made. It's people, products and services that you have to keep an eye on. Oxford American dictionary describes selling as "to persuade someone of the merits of".

Teens are always trying to sell their parents on their independence, asking, "Why can't I stay out until 2 AM, all my friends do?" While the parents are trying to sell their teens on their authority, " 2 AM is too late, I want you home by midnight!"

Churches and other charitable organizations must sell their members and donors on why they need to continue to financially support the causes of the organization and not take their support elsewhere.

When you're on a first date or a job interview you're selling yourself on the strength of your character, skills and abilities. (Most of the characters that have tried to date my daughters have been horrible salesmen!)

A great preacher or public speaker must learn how to sell his ideas effectively if he/she wants to win their audience over to the topic being preached.

The first sale you must make is to yourself. I had to sell myself on the idea that I could be in music ministry full time. I initially didn't think that I was good enough.

I even had to sell myself on writing this book. I know that there are thousands of books being published every year on every subject imaginable, so why should I write just another one. I sold myself on the fact that there are people out there that for whatever reason are going to pick up this book in particular, and find the encouragement to begin to change their lives.

Read a book on selling, even if it's not your career. It will teach you how to get your ideas across from the other person' s perspective —handle objections, negotiate effectively and close the deal.

Two great books are *The Slight Edge* by Jeff Olsen and *Think and Grow Rich* by Napoleon Hill. You don't even have to be in the sales business to enjoy these powerful resources.

5. **No excuses**
You can make excuses or you could live your life walking by faith in power, but you can't do both. If you say, "I can," you're right. If you say, "I can't," you're also right. Choose to say "I CAN" and then stick to it.

6. **Fence sitting is not optional**
Our relationship with God cannot be some lukewarm, halfhearted, religious attempt at serving Him. To get your power back, you've got to be connected to God through Jesus Christ by the power of the Spirit.

God goes before you and orders your steps when you put Him first. His will, His way no exceptions. Jesus did nothing without first praying and seeking the will of the Father. Don't waste your life doing things your own way and then wonder where God is when your world caves in.

My wife and I have a dear friend that we've known for over twenty years. To protect her identity, I'll call her Linda.

Linda was in an abusive marriage for many years, feeling trapped as she raised her children in New York City. She went to church, sang in the choir, and was involved in outreach ministries, but any joy she felt in raising her children and serving God was erased by the emotional and physical abuse she received when her husband came home.

After a painful and emotionally draining divorce, she moved upstate New York, trying to rebuild her life and escape the reminders of how her fairytale marriage turned into a horrible nightmare.

As time goes by, and with her children now all grown up, she meets a handsome, kind and giving man at the place where she works. This is just the kind of man she needed. Everything is going just wonderful. Maybe a few little bumps in the road here and there but nothing that can't be worked out.

They soon marry but on the very night of their honeymoon, his personality seemed to totally transform as he screamed curses at his new bride for no apparent reason. Linda was dazed but determined to make this marriage work. She constantly lived under the fear of his ferocious outbursts and anger.

Although her children were grown and before they were married, they agreed not to have more children, he forced her to quit her job and have two more children.

Now unemployed with two young boys, he began to hit Linda and continued to berate her. He would give her very little money to take care of the home and children. She was virtually a prisoner in her own home. He began having affairs with other women, and dared her to try to leave or do anything about it. He made her to feel worthless. She kept thinking that if she could find a job, who would hire her? How would she take care of the children?

She often thought of leaving him but with no money and two little boys, she couldn't face the thought of going through a second failed marriage. Maybe God would turn his heart. Maybe he'll see the error of his ways. Maybe it's all her fault, but it was not meant to be.

The final straw came when he started bringing women home and having sex with them in their bed. Linda took her boys and fled to her married daughters home.

She felt like she couldn't breathe. There she was – embarrassed, devastated and humiliated, she lived with this secret until she could bear it no longer. Linda found refuge in my wife's women's prayer group. The prayers, support and testimonies of the other women, some who had been through similar situations strengthened her.

After finding the courage to file for divorce, she told her attorney she doesn't want anything from him, she just wanted to see this chapter of her life behind her. Linda told her attorney she was a Christian and didn't want to fight anymore. Although she desperately needed it, she didn't want to ask for any kind of financial support. Besides, as far as she knew, he didn't have much money anyway.

The attorney respected Linda's beliefs, but told her that she won't tell Linda how to pray, if she won't tell her how to practice law. You see the truth is, at times in order to get your power back, to keep your faith strong; you've got to fight.

The proceedings went forward and the attorney went to work. The attorney went inside the conference room to negotiate a settlement with the attorneys who represented Linda's husband, while Linda sat outside the conference room a bundle of nerves – praying.

After what seemed like forever, the negotiations come to an end. Linda looks up as she watches her smiling attorney approaching her. Not only had the attorney found out that Linda's husband had hidden large sums of money during the marriage, but that she was also going to receive a high five figure lump sum settlement as well as monthly child support.

One week prior, embarrassed, Linda couldn't afford to cash a twenty-five dollar check at the bank because she didn't have enough in her account to cover it. Now, she has enough to move out of her daughter's home, find a place of her own and make a fresh start with her two little boys.

She now realizes that her low self-esteem and her need to have a companion in her life in order to make her feel like she was being loved, drove her to seemingly strong but very abusive men.

Today, just a couple of years later, Linda is successfully raising her sons. She works full time for an international Christian missions organization. She's a leader in the women's prayer group, and is one of the heads of the prayer and Bible study at her church. She is also a mentor to young girls and a passionate soul winner sharing the love of Christ with everyone she meets.

She had once lost her joy—her peace—her self-respect—her sense of purpose. But she got it back.

I leave you with a great and timely song written by my friend Keith Laws. I recorded this song on my newest CD entitled *The Faith Life.*

Sometimes we hold on a little longer than we should
Letting go can be hard, but it's sometimes for our good
The fear of what's ahead, sometimes makes
us fall behind
You can see the times are changing
But pretend that you're so blind
You'll never really know just what the future holds
But we know, God holds us in His hand
So by faith, we must climb into the boat
And follow His command

I Got It Back!

Launch out into the deep
Let your faith take you somewhere
That you've never been before
Launch out into the deep
Let your faith make you fly
Let your faith make you soar
Launch out, launch out into the deep

It's time to wake up, and make our dreams come
true
Time is always moving, and it will not wait for you
The fear inside your mind, can quench the fire in
your heart
Sometimes where you end, is where
God wants to start
It's never easy when you're walking out by faith
Everything seems so different and new
But if we only learn to see with eyes of faith
We could see life in a different view

Launch out into the deep
Let your faith take you somewhere
That you've never been before
Launch out into the deep
Let your faith make you fly
Let your faith make you soar
Launch out, launch out into the deep
So much for you awaiting
So stop procrastinating
Close your eyes,
Just take a leap

Launch out into the deep
Let your faith take you somewhere
That you've never been before
Launch out into the deep
Let your faith make you fly
Let your faith make you soar
Launch out, launch out into the deep

Chapter Six
GIVE IT AWAY!
(MULTIPLY)

God doesn't only bless us so that we can feel better. He also blesses us so that we can serve better. He loves giving good things to His children. He wants us to give also. I don't believe I'll ever fully understand how increase comes into our lives when we give, I do know that it does. I am who I am and what I am in life today because someone gave to me. Some gave hope and encouragement, another forgiveness and truth. And still others gave their time and attention or their patience and understanding; while many other gave love and laughter. And some even gave money and material possessions.

Think about it. Wherever you are in life, you didn't get there solely by yourself. And if you need to grow some more, as we all do, it will be someone that God has placed into your path to help you on your journey.

The Bible says that God gives seed to the sower. I imagine that the implied idea of this scripture is also that if you stop sowing, you don't get any more seed from Him.

Notice that it says He *gives* seed to the sower. God will give to you supernaturally when you give.

Not only that, God gives back to you in abundance over and above what you give to others. This is a principal that is for everyone – those who believe and those who don't. God blesses our life when we give.

Some athletes, rock stars and movie stars have become well known for their giving. The work of celebrities like Magic Johnson, Bill Gates, Tiger Woods, Oprah Winfrey, Bono and Angelina Jolie are known around the world for their giving and compassion to the less fortunate. All very talented, but I believe that part of the reason that their "cups are running over" is that they had a giving heart even when they had no money, so giving is in their souls.

Now some may say, "well, if I had their talent or money, I could give too!" True giving is not only based on money and talent. I can only find six reasons that hinder giving. They are, poverty—selfishness—mismanagement—uncaring—lack of faith and cheap. Even these are poor excuses for not giving.

Begin with what you do have. You see, you don't have to have a lot of money, but everybody, no matter who you are has something that God has given you in abundance. And whatever you have in abundance, you must give it away.

The act of giving itself is powerful. First of all, it takes all the focus off of you. Selfish people are small minded and devalued. Small minded because you can't grow if your whole world revolves around you. Devalued because you are of no significance to the people, community and world that sustains you. Selfish people receive back from life, exactly what they put into it. Which is a great segway to the 70's hit song, *Nothing From Nothing Leaves Nothing.* Our character reflects what we have invested in ourslves, with God and with others.

Givers give into life and something supernatural happens. You don't just get back what you've given, but you get it back in multiples. One of the unique promises of the Bible is that the more you give, the more you receive. It may not always be in material possessions, but in spiritual and eternal rewards.

My ministry career has never been based on whether I have had a hit record or not. Neither is it based on whether I'm getting massive radio airplay. I've always wanted that, but it never happened for me. I don't have a manager neither do I have a booking agent. Maybe one day I will.

No pity party here! I've seen artists come and I've seen them go. However, for over sixteen years now, churches, promoters and organizations have invited me and are still inviting me to come speak and perform in concerts and worship events literally all over the world. I've sung before millions through live events and television. God has given me favor over the years with TBN, Integrity Music and hundreds of churches, conferences, and Christian leaders internationally.

I know there are several reasons why God has opened these doors. But if I can pinpoint it to one main thing, it would be giving. If I had never volunteered for the choirs at Pilgrim Cathedral and later at the Brooklyn Tabernacle, I would have never known the acceptance from the people when I sang and I wouldn't know that God could use me this way. I didn't really have a lot of self-confidence in my ability. There are so many talented singers who could sing rings around me. But I really don't worry about that. Because I do know that little becomes much when God blesses it.

I didn't always have the money, but I gave everything I could at the time to my church family and the people God brought in my path. I've made some mistakes. I didn't always give, as I should have. And most of the time, what I gave was not noticed by a lot of people. But God sees it, and has rewarded me according to His good pleasure for my life. That's why today, more than ever, I still believe in sacrificial giving.

To see my wife in a powerful women's ministry, my children and daughter-in-law serving God, and three of them heavily involved in ministry is a reflection of the power of multiplication.

When you give, you have the ability to greatly affect somebody's life and God loves cheerful givers. But also, and never forget this, giving makes you a powerful person. There are people with the ability to take resources as well as intangibles and turn them into someone's answer to prayer. That literally reflects the image of Almighty God. Now that's priceless!

If you're a patient person, give understanding
Get virtue back!

If you're a joyful person, give laughter
Get pleasure back!

If you're strong, give a hand
Get appreciation back!

If you're enthusiastic, light somebody's fire
Get passion back!

If you're a good listener, lend an ear
Get discernment back!

If you're a talker, speak life
Get encouragement back!

If you've been wronged, give forgiveness
Get your power back!

I think you see where I'm going with this. Give your tithes, offerings and donations. Give your absolute best. There is more to this life than what money can buy. Should you expect something in return for your giving? Absolutely! God made some promises in Psalm 41:1-3 to those of us who give.

Oh, the joys of those who are kind to the poor.
The LORD rescues them in times of trouble.
The LORD protects them .
and keeps them alive.
He gives them prosperity
and rescues them from their enemies.
The LORD nurses them when they are sick
and eases their pain and discomfort.

When you give to someone and you see how it touches his or her life, the payoff can even be greater than any material thing you could personally receive. To be part of a project that feeds the hungry, builds homes for the homeless or digs wells in Africa is a great and life changing experience. Giving to a church or organization that is making a social and spiritual impact in the lives of the community — discovering cures for diseases, or protecting those who have been abandoned and abused is not even an option. Giving is our spiritual responsibility.

I don't agree with those who say we should not expect anything in return. The return may not always be something that you can hold in your hand. And for those who are not moved by seeing someone's despair turn to joy, then they need to deal with the coldness of their heart.

Another thing, always be a gracious receiver. Many years ago a Pastor was telling me how much he enjoyed the song I sang that night and how it really connected with him. As was my usual habit, I started telling him how I was a little hoarse and that I almost forgot the words to the second verse and I was flat when I tried to hit the high note. All of a sudden, he put up his hand as though to stay "stop" and said to me, "just say thank you." I don't know whether I had too much pride or too low self esteem back then, but I no longer give excuses – just gratitude.

Jesus was going through a village, heading towards Jerusalem, when ten lepers stood at a distance, crying out, "Jesus, Master, have mercy on us!"

Leprosy is often called "a living death" because of the many horrifying and debilitating effects on the human body. (Visit *www.leprosy.org*) At the time there was no cure. It left people deformed and hopeless for the rest of their lives. Lepers were abandoned by their friends and families and forced to live by themselves in leper colonies.

Jesus looked at them and said, "Go show yourselves to the priests." As they went, their leprosy disappeared.

When he saw that he was healed, one of them came back to Jesus, shouting, "Praise God, I'm healed!" He fell face down on the ground at Jesus' feet, thanking Him for what He had done. This man was a Samaritan.

Jesus asked, "Didn't I heal ten men? Where are the other nine? Does only this foreigner return to give glory to God?" And Jesus said to the man, "Stand up and go. Your faith has made you well." (Luke 17:14-16) Interesting. Jesus gave healing and expected gratitude. When we give and when we receive with gratitude, it opens the gates for God's flow of love and blessings into our lives.

Mark 4:24, 25 says, *"Listen carefully to what I am saying—and be wary of the shrewd advice that tells you how to get ahead in the world on your own. Giving, not getting, is the way. Generosity begets generosity. Stinginess impoverishes."* So desire to grow in your giving. To grow you must:

106

Have the right priority
What is the reason you give? Giving to satisfy your ego is not giving according to God's plan.

Make an ongoing plan
Plan to give regularly, not just one time. One time giving for a one-time solution is not being a giver, but being a gambler.

Cut your expenses
Eliminate things in your life that hinder giving. Bad debt, spending what you can't afford and wasting money on things of no value hinders your giving.

Walk In the Spirit
You can't help everybody and you sure can't change the world by yourself. Let the Spirit of God guide you in your giving.

I pray that this book has helped you to see yourself the way that our heavenly Father sees you. I hope that when doubts and trials rock your world, that something in this book will remind you of the powerful person you truly are in Christ. You've come to the end of the book, but this is not the end of your potential, your contribution, and your life. To truly be able to say that *I Got It Back!* and to continue in the favor and direction of God, you have to be a giver.

I leave you with the words of the Apostle Paul's intensely personal letter to the church in Corinth. The church at Corinth had been a weak church surrounded by idolatry and immorality. They had struggled with their Christian faith and lifestyle.

After some time, Paul realized that most of the believers in Corinth had taken his previous letters to
heart. They were now beginning to mature in their
faith. He writes:

And God will generously provide all you need.
Then you will always have everything you need and
plenty left over to share with others. As the Scriptures say,

"Godly people give generously to the poor.
Their good deeds will never be forgotten.

"For God is the one who gives seed to the farmer
and then bread to eat. In the same way, he will give
you many opportunities to do good, and he will pro-
duce a great harvest of generosity in you.

Yes, you will be enriched so that you can give even
more generously. And when we take your gifts to
those who need them, they will break out in thanks-
giving to God. So two good things will happen—the
needs of the Christians in Jerusalem will be met,
and they will joyfully express their thanksgiving to
God. You will be glorifying God through your gener-
ous gifts. For your generosity to them will prove that
you are obedient to the Good News of Christ." (2
Corinthians 9:8-13)

The 'LIFE' Book

Chapter One

LET'S SET THE RECORD STRAIGHT!

This is not easy for me to confess. It never is when you finally realize that what you prayed about, got frustrated about, almost threw in the towel about and blamed God for, was something that was never going to happen anyway. Well, not the way you wanted it to happen. No matter how frustrated you got. NO matter how hard you prayed.

Identify three things that you prayed desperately about, but it either didn't come to pass the way you thought, or has not happened at all.

Have any of these things made you feel as if **God has forgotten** about you? Have you fallen into **depression**? Self-pity? Has it caused you to **see the world**, yourself and others in a **negative way**?

Myth 1 – If I truly have faith, I shouldn't feel afraid. There are times that you will be afraid.**What do you fear most?** As you answer this make sure you are honest with yourself.

Is your fear a healthy one? There are some fears that we have that keep us, emotionally, spiritually and physically safe.

Even people we consider great have fears. Therefore, it is *not* having fear that is the most destructive to our lives – it is how we react to fear that is most important. So I ask you, how do you react or respond when you are afraid?

There is a way to minimize unwarranted fears. Start seeking wise counsel and avoid wishful thinking.

What steps can you take to overcome that fear?

Join a small informal group of faith builders or find a prayer partner who knows how to connect with God. Don't isolate – insulate. Remember, God will give you the courage and boldness to walk through your all of your fears!

Name three faith building sources you can become a part of.

Name three people or places where you can receive wise counsel.

At the same time, start developing wisdom and in-dependence so that you are not solely dependent on the opinions of others. I suggest reading the book of Proverbs. What are some other ways can you develop wisdom?

Are you only thinking about what you wish will hap-pen instead of taking the necessary steps to make them come to pass?

Wishful thinking is a prescription for a defeated life. Instead move in the power that God has given you. Instead of wishful thinking, write the top five things that you 'wish' you could see happen in your life below.

A vision without a strategy is just a fantasy. So write out the first three things that you need to do in order to see what you are wishing for.

Myth 2 – I'm not worthy.
Who told you that? *"I thank you, High God –*
you're breathtaking! Body and soul, I am mar-
velously made! I worship in adoration – what a
creation!" **(Psalm 139:14)**

Pause for a moment; reflect in your memory and
pinpoint where this lie came from. Identify a person
or a specific place that planted this thought into your
spirit?

In your Bible, read and meditate on Jeremiah 29:11.
Rehearse this scripture over and over until it begins
to take hold of you more than thoughts of unworthi-
ness.

Through the power of the Spirit of God, I come into
agreement with you as He makes this thought come
alive in your heart.

Myth 3 – I can't face rejection. *"Be strong in the Lord and in the power of His might."* **(Ephesians 6:10) No one likes rejection. However, replace feelings of rejection with feelings of strength in order for you to lead an empowered life.**

Describe a specific event where you felt rejected. How did you handle the rejection at that moment?

How do you handle rejection now?

What can you do to continue to develop your focus and your self-worth?

Do you have 'toxic' people around you?

What steps do you need to take so that you feel supported and not rejected?

Myth 4 – I'm not a strong person.
Just because you're imperfect doesn't mean that
you're powerless. The truth is, being strong re-
ally means becoming strong. None of us are born
strong, but we gain strength as we develop over
time.

Do you consider yourself a strong person? If not, why? If yes, explain how you feel your strength has helped or hurt you over the years.

Name three people, places or things that sap your strength and also name three people, places or things that give you strength.

Myth 5 – I don't know what to do.
Get connected to the Source who is the Spirit of God. Seek wise counsel and don't live in a vacuum.

Write down the three biggest challenges that you are facing at this time in your life.

Who are your spiritual, financial, and emotional resources?

A mentor is someone you connect with that you can draw wisdom from. You don't have to even personally know them. Their books, sermons or experiences help give you insight. Who are your mentors?

What do you believe God is leading you to do?

Note: Don't overlook the practical solution or process that God may lead you through to see change.

Myth 6 – I'll be misunderstood.
Yes, you will, but you were not put on this earth to win a popularity contest. Your first priority must be to know and to do what God's will is for you.

Are you afraid of being misunderstood? If so, why do you think that being misunderstood is so important to you?

God doesn't remove our fears. We remove them through faith and taking by action. You have the power, the faith and the courage inside of you to get you through. Faith is the key, not wishful thinking. Wishful thinking provides absolutely no basis for victory in the end.

How does wishful thinking and faith differ?

How has this affected your life in the past?

Give an example of wishful thinking in your own life.

At this time in your life, on a scale of 1 through 10, would you say your faith is strong or weak? Why? (1 being no faith, and 10 being great faith)

I believe that we face four dominant fears, the fear of failure, the fear of rejection, the fear of not being successful and the fear of success. It is important for you to know which one of these fears has the most impact on you life.

Rank the following four dominant fears, 1 through, 4 based on their impact on your life.

Explain your reason for choosing #1 and #4.

Basic Training for Overcoming Fear
God doesn't want us to only feel inspired. He wants us to be transformed by having our minds renewed. The mind is the battleground where the seeds of fear and depression are planted.

Write down four scriptures that instruct us to allow the Spirit of God to transform or influence our mind.

Take responsibility for your own life. Just because you have been a victim does not mean that you have to make that experience a permanent residence in your life.

Write down some of the things that you need to do different in order to face and overcome the challenges you are facing today.

Personal growth is the key to prosperity. It's amazing how people spend so much money on things that are not going to prosper them. You see, new and fresh ideas will begin to take shape in your mind and the blessings will begin to flow as you begin to act on your newfound knowledge.

What can you do to enhance your personal growth and development? (i.e. books, classes, tapes, etc.)

"Wealthy people have big libraries. Poor people have big televisions." Which of these descriptions fit you, and what must you do or stop doing to increase your wealth?

If you find it difficult to effectively communicate your thoughts or feelings in a confrontational situation, you will always feel like you're on the losing side.

Do you feel as though you're a good communicator?

If not, where do you feel you need the most help in order to be able to communicate more effectively?

Chapter Two

DEEPENING YOUR RELATIONSHIP WITH GOD

The life of a Christian is not exempt from tragedy. But that does not mean that a Christian should live their life in constant worry and defeat because of circumstances.

How do you typically cope when tragedy strikes?

What can you do to find peace with God in times of tragedy or distress?

Financial prosperity does not come from just putting money in the offering basket. There are other things that you must do as well.

What is your personal definition of financial prosperity?

Name ay least four things you must do other than tithes and offerings to increase your finances.

Everything we own belongs to God. So when we give out tithes and offerings, it shows God that He can trust us with the resources He has provided for us. However, giving becomes problematic if you're an impulsive spender, in debt, earn low wages, or mismanage money through lack of wisdom and education.

What are the stumbling blocks to your financial prosperity?

What can you do to increase your income or lower your debt?

Persistent worry is detrimental to the believer because it replaces persistent prayer. Worry doesn't cause God to move. However, God will move heaven and earth when we pray in faith according to His will. (Luke 18:18)

Write a prayer making your requests to God just as if you were saying it aloud. Make it as long or short as you would like...but don't hold back.

(prayer continued)

After you write the prayer, go to the Bible and find the scriptures that confirm that your prayer is according to God's will and write them down.

What do you need to cut out, rearrange, ignore or manage better so that you can make prayer apart of your everyday life?

Many times when we don't know what to do, we pray for a miracle. Miracles do happen, but we must also seek the Lord for wisdom and direction.

Write down six things you need wisdom or direction for.

Take one week and pray each day asking God to reveal His plan to you and to give you the steps in order to see that plan fulfilled. Get a notebook and document what you receive from Him.

Don't be afraid to share your heart with God. He already knows more than you can tell Him!

134

We should all aspire to leadership. It doesn't matter if you've never led a Fortune 500 corporation or an international ministry, but you need to learn to lead *you*!

So I want you to find one book on leadership, (I suggest *The 21 Irrefutable Laws* by John Maxwell). Take this book and let it begin to develop leadership skills in you. Most people live their lives as though they have very few options. As a leader you'll think differently about yourself and the world around you. This is your life and you are the leader of it!

Unresolved and unrepentant sin can steal your joy. (Read Psalm 51:8)

Do you have unrepentant or unresolved sin in your life? Bad habits, destructive behavior, bitterness, and all the things that hinder the process of becoming whole spiritually, physically and emotionally. Let's pray together!

Father, I receive you wholly into my life. I need you to help me to deal with and overcome the things of the past and even the present, that have kept me from being the person you created me to be. Renew my mind. Restore me and fill me with the power of Your Spirit. Give me greater understanding and wisdom as I grow in your love. As I begin a new day on this journey of grace, thank you for being my Guide, my Father, and my Friend.

In Jesus' Name, amen.

Doing things that you enjoy help will bring joy into your life as well.

Perhaps life has become so busy and overwhelming that you have neglected some of the little things that bring you joy. Write down ten things that bring you joy.

A very important part of enjoying everyday life is experiencing the presence of God.

Four ways to invite the presence of God are: Praise—Music—Meditation—Serving

What is it that you can thank and praise God for today?

What song can you sing or music you play that helps you to encounter God?

Name five promises of God from the Bible that can become part of your daily meditation?

What act of service can you perform that expresses your love for God and ministry to others?

Our minds are filled with images and experiences of the past. All the "data" is stored in your mind. So you must realize that the filter of your mind might be clogged.

What is clogging your filter?

What steps can you take to begin to clean the filter and start thinking differently?

Without faith it is impossible to please God. To deepen your relationship with God, you must have faith. It is important to have faith, but it is also important to watch out for traps that can sabotage your faith.

The faith traps are: **Hype Driven Faith Trap, Double Minded Faith Trap and Fragmented Faith Trap.** Which 'faith trap' is affecting your life and how is it affecting it?

Chapter Three
Discover Your Passion
(Getting Unstuck)

Rich or poor, educated or illiterate, focused or clueless, at the final days of our lives we don't have to look far to find our passions. Our true passions will find us.

What passions have you lacked the courage to pursue?

When must you do to break away from the pack and start doing what your heart tells you to do?

Knowing that passions can change, how do you think your passions have changed yesterday and today?

Are you having trouble identifying your passion? Then ask yourself this question. *"What would I love to do even if I were not being paid?"*

Another way to identify your passion is by paying attention to the things you do. When you do them, do you feel God's favor in the process?

Reaching out to others is another way to help get 'unstuck' in life. It helps you get your mind off you and on the business of living and being productive. What opportunities are before you where you can impact a child, an adult or a family's life?

Chapter Four

Next Level Belief!

Describe 10 qualities about yourself that don't mention your job title, or your responsibilities. Such as honest, good listener, etc.

Do you see yourself as cynical, skeptical, or trusting about people and life in general and why do you see yourself this way?

Visualize It
**The first step to 'next level' belief is visualizing it
without your eyes. See it in your mind. Feel it in
your heart. Receive it in your spirit.**

Write down how or where you want to see yourself
12 months from now.

Confirm it in your spirit
The next step is to confirm it in your spirit, which is your human spirit joining with God's Holy Spirit. It is God's will becoming your will.

Write down what commitments you plan to make everyday to feed your spirit and connect with God.

Create it with your actions
The third and final step is to create it with your actions. Take small steps or big steps. It doesn't matter, just get moving and begin creating momentum.

What is your plan and what steps are you going to take. As you write it down, be specific and put a timetable on when you are going to take these actions.

Chapter Five

GET Going!

Procrastination will kill your future. Stop waiting for a miracle. God will bring miracles into your life according to His will. Get going and start living the faith life. Make this your year of living with focus and intention.

Name five things you have been putting off or procrastinating about. (Go ahead, write it now!)

What's stopping you from moving forward?

Anticipate Victory
Failure is a part of the process of life, but to have constant thoughts of failure is self-defeating.

Do you always feel like something is going to go wrong?

What's the worst thing that can happen?

What's the best thing that can happen?

Begin with the end in mind
Develop a blueprint for how you will get to the place where you want to be in life.

Write out a detailed strategy of how you are going to initiate change to become the person you want to be.

**Become a student of personal development
Become a person of influence by overcoming
fear, rejection and people's opinions of you.**

Write down some specific things you can do to im-
prove yourself?

Sell, sell, and sell!
You must learn how to sell in order to get your power back!

Write out one paragraph that can be used to sell or present your idea and concept to others.

Chapter Six

Give It Away! (Multiply)

I don't believe I'll ever fully understand how increase comes into our lives when we give, but I do know that it does. I am who *I am* and what I am in life today because someone gave.

Name three things that hinder your giving?

What three things can you give to organizations or individuals this month without looking for repayment? This could be money, encouragement, clothes, food, or whatever you choose.

Begin giving what you have. No matter who you are, God has given you something in abundance.

You must have the right motive when you give. What are your reasons for giving?

In order to give on an ongoing basis, you must plan ahead. Write out your weekly or monthly giving plan.

Cut your expenses.
Is there anything you can eliminate from your budget or temporarily sacrifice so that you will be able to freely give?

Write down 12 things that have been given to you throughout your life that you are thankful for?

Notes _____

_____

_____

_____

_____

_____

_____

_____

_____

_____

_____

_____

_____

_____

_____

_____

Notes _____

Notes _____

Notes _____

Notes

Notes _____

Notes _____

Notes _____

Notes _____

Notes _____

_____

_____

_____

_____

_____

_____

_____

_____

_____

_____

_____

_____

_____

_____

Notes

Notes

Notes _____

_____

_____

_____

_____

_____

_____

_____

_____

_____

_____

_____

_____

_____

_____

_____

Notes

Notes _____

Notes